The United States Of Theocracy

The Christian Taliban Assault on Our Freedom

By
Janet K. Humphreys, Ph.D.

Rev. Dates: 1/21/2016 and 3/01/2019
ISBN 13: 978-1523318483
Library of Congress Number: 2013919766

Awards:

Hollywood Book Festival, Honorable Mention, 2014
Florida Book Festival, Honorable Mention, 2015

Hollywood Book Festival Review

This is a chilling book. It is the story of an educated woman who takes a job in the prison system, believing that her professional skills and insight will help society by diagnosing and treating the root causes of criminal activity. But she soon realizes that the bureaucratic nightmare she has stepped into is not just incompetence or malicious office politics, but may conceal something far more insidious. In "The United States of Theocracy: The Christian Taliban Assault on Our Freedom," Dr. Janet Humphreys chronicles her illuminating discoveries in a fast-paced read that is part autobiography, part political analysis, and part non-fiction investigation of a system that appears almost insane. As a dedicated psychologist who wants to do her job the right way and help the people she's there to serve, Humphreys instead runs into roadblock after roadblock, as strange, controlling characters thwart her attempts at doing the right thing and even go so far as to ignore basic human decency in the workplace.

While the early part of the book is focused on an individual's confrontations with an unyielding system, this book is much more than a rant against the machine. It exposes a prison system whose sole purpose seems to be preserving its own existence instead of rehabilitation and treatment. Inmates are found to be in jail for such mundane things as traffic tickets, missed appointments and minor civil infractions, clogging the prison system and leaving little time for serious and necessary analysis and examination of dangerous people who have problems that need grave psychological help.

Stranger still is the slow realization by Humphreys that fundamentalist Christians working with her may be undercutting her efforts simply because she holds different views. Even a simple declaration by Humphreys that evolution and Christianity are not incompatible seems to blow the minds of her fundamentalist co-workers, whose rigid adherence to their self-righteous beliefs do, in fact, resemble the Christian version of Afghanistan's Taliban.

Humphreys takes the focus off her personal confrontations for the last third of the book, working hard to explain how to cure the ills she perceives in the world. From prison and Social Security reform to the monitoring of law enforcement and the education system, she offers up practical solutions that rely on a humane and reasoned view of the world. Her common-sense approach is alien to those from her past and readers will no doubt agree that their inflexible approach is leading this country down the wrong path, particularly in an age where the economic whirlwind is creating anger and bitterness among those who are having trouble adjusting.

"As long as our economy is distressed and jobs are scarce, young men and women will continue to enter our voluntary armed forces and help out the rich by fighting their oil wars for them," Humphreys writes to explain the strange attitudes she encounters.

"Fundamentalism encourages putting the blame on women for the struggles of men, rather than on our wealthy rulers, where it justly belongs."

Humphreys is doing a public service with her analysis of an alarming and growing fundamentalism. "It is said that when evil is brought into the light, it will lose its power," she concludes. Books like this go a long way toward ensuring that the disinfectant of knowledge may yet help people escape from the encroaching darkness.

To my mother, Betty,
Who believed that education could bring peace
To the world,
And
To my father, Bill,
Who struggled to keep peace in our family.

Thanks to:

My ever-patient friends who listened tirelessly as I tried to figure out what was going on in my life

The prison staff and prisoners who helped me navigate the difficult maze that is a prison

The staff of the Juvenile Justice Department, who shared their own frustrations with corruption in the State of Florida

The many applicants for social security disability, who shared their stories with me

The staff at the Division of Disability Determinations at the Florida Department of Health who kept me afloat post-prison

Those who dared to investigate the Christian Taliban at all its levels and write about their experiences, especially Kathryn Joyce, Katherine Stewart, Chris Hedges, Jeff Sharlet, and Michelle Goldberg

And last, but not least,

The many fundamentalists, who through their very bad behavior, made me aware of the great threat they pose to our society.

Table of Contents

Forward

They say you should expect seven obstacles in your way every time you set a goal. In my case, it's more like a hundred. A psychic once told me that everything's harder for me and that I have to do everything by myself. Yes, I'm alone. And yes, I've consulted psychics. You see, when it seems all your luck is bad, you look for explanations on a different level

I've read *The Secret*, and long before that, I read Wayne Dyer, Deepak Chopra, Abraham, and a host of others with their own versions of that "secret." Yet in the past few years, I've attracted one calamity after another. I'm not a person who tries to hurt others. I've spent my life in the helping business.

Don't get me wrong. I do believe you have to cling to your goal to get what you want as *The Secret* and all those who came before said. But I think that's simplistic. Who was it who said, "If you want to make God laugh, tell her your plan?" I think if your goal for yourself is consistent with God's goal for you, the *secret* works. And I think God's goal is not necessarily for us to have an easy life – there'd be no purpose in coming here if it were. Most of us don't consciously make "maximum learning experiences" our goal.

Karma might make sense of my life. Of course, that's presupposing I've had other lives in which I was a horrible person, and I have some difficulty conceiving of myself as being totally different at my core. I know I haven't been perfect, but I haven't been that bad in this life.

I was so attracted to all those new age theories. Wishful thinking – what a wonderful concept! Let me hold the thought! There's always some reason this stuff doesn't work. Mostly, I'm told it has to do with my attitude.

Yet my friends used to tell me that I always seemed happy – in spite of whatever calamity was befalling me at the moment. I'm always looking for an explanation as to how what seems to be a current calamity is actually helping me in some way. I'm still trying to believe that everything that happens is for my good. When a contractor brought thin wood strips for the outside of my house instead of the thicker, wider, hardiboard strips I asked for (and paid for) I let it go. Others may think of this as passivity, but in the end, I liked the result – my house looks more like a little cottage, which suits my surroundings. When another contractor bought 22 boxes of extra tile and left them out in the rain so I couldn't return them, I trusted I'd have something to do with them, and it turned out they made a beautiful kitchen countertop. I would have never thought of using the same tiles for the countertop if this hadn't happened. I like the idea of reverse paranoia – everything happens for my good. I won't let go of that one – it's the only thing that keeps me sane these days.

I also like the idea of earth being our school. Some of us choose to learn a lot through repeated challenges. It gives me at least some sense of control over the seeming chaos of my life if I've somehow chosen this mess. Maybe I had some part in making the plan before I came here. I'm hoping I've chosen this many challenges because this is my last time around here on earth. While I'm here though, the feeling I like best is being able to help people. It makes me think there is some purpose to my existence. I have an 80 year old friend who is afraid of not having fulfilled her purpose on earth. As I get older, I'm sharing this feeling. I feel I need to hurry now to accomplish everything I need to do here. I'm moved to write, hoping this will help others make sense of their lives.

Since I've moved to North Florida, I've become more interested in the nature of evil than how to raise my consciousness. Just making it through each day has been such a challenge that I haven't had time to strive for much beyond survival. I've always had my challenges, but they've come in hyper speed in the past few years. I'm just grateful they've appeared in every facet of my life so I don't have time to dwell on any one disaster.

I think there are a lot of us who are not at all perfect, but have good intentions and somehow end up with an awful lot of challenges in life. I think people who try to live their lives according to what they think is right and good generally do have a lot of problems. There are so many people out there who seem to take offense at people who will not join them in their corrupt ways.

In the midst of this chaos, I decided to build a house. I would be my own contractor and save myself some money. Oh yeah – save some money. Only it didn't turn out that way because nobody I hired did what they had said they would do – so then I had to hire someone else to finish the job. Sometimes, that person didn't finish the job either, so I had to hire yet another person to finish their job. Sometimes, they just didn't show up to start with which, of course, cost me more time, which ultimately, was even more frustrating because I insisted on setting deadlines for getting things done. With neighbors and relatives asking for weekly accounts of my progress and pointing out the chaos in which I lived, l felt pressured to meet their lofty expectations. So, I set the timelines, which the laborers I hired were intent on defying.

The other problem I've encountered in dealing with construction workers is my need to be kind to people. As a psychologist, I know that people with antisocial personalities see kindness as weakness and fear, yet I persisted in doing my best to help the people who came my way, and they took advantage of my good nature. Obviously, while not all construction workers are antisocial personalities any more than all car mechanics are antisocial, somehow I managed to attract mostly those who were. They gave me a lot of practice in not responding in kind to bad behavior.

All of us hurt other people we don't mean to hurt as we plow through life largely unconscious and unaware. However, there are people who feel justified in hurting others and intentionally do so. I think maybe evil boils down to intention. These are the people who've surrounded me the past few years more than usual in my life. Working in prisons perhaps allowed me greater exposure to this craziness than most people.

I was raised in liberal Christian churches where God was viewed as loving and forgiving. It was acknowledged that the Bible was God's word as interpreted by the men who wrote it down – men who perhaps had an interest in slanting that word somewhat to meet their own needs. Intelligent people need to shift through the many contradictions of the Bible and salvage the truth therein.

I had read of less enlightened Christian churches that focus on retribution rather than forgiveness, and believe that the Bible in all its contradictions is the literal word of God. However, I could never have imagined the consequences of being a divorced, educated woman living around people with these beliefs before I moved to North Florida.

I understand the concept of possession. The movie, "The Exorcist," portrayed that well enough. What's harder to understand are people who just seem evil (or insane as Tolle might say) – not writing on the floor possessed. I met people while working in prison who got great delight out of causing people pain – and these weren't mostly the prisoners! They seem to share in common a narcissism that blinds them in many ways to the needs of others – or allows them to think that no one else's needs matter. Wait a minute! That actually does sound like some of those new age theories. Abraham likes to tell people to "mind your own business" and Hawkins encourages people to focus on their own evolution of consciousness, saying they're not responsible for anyone else. Unlike many of these popular new age theories, I believe a social consciousness is a good thing. I don't believe we're just here for ourselves and this is why I feel compelled to share my story.

We all survived Mayan predictions of an end of an era in December 2012. What I find interesting is the Hopi prediction, which suggests we have come to a fork in the road. We have choices to make as a collective. The choices range from complete destruction and loss of sunlight, to less severe circumstances (providing that corruption and greed has not already gone too far). Hopefully, we can wake up to the lies we've been accepting as truth and create a new world.

The problem I have had since I left my job in prison is that the evil I met up with in prison seems to have followed me, and the effect has been so pervasive in my life that I find myself at this point having trouble being happy about the opportunity I've been given to learn from it. It's brought me to seriously consider the whole fate thing. I can accept my circumstances easier if it was all written before I came here. And there was that psychic I went to who read my aura when I was 23 years old (my desperation came early) and she predicted all this mess. Then there's that whole school of scientists who also believe our programming is stored in our aura.

As I said before, my life only makes sense if I'm supposed to be here in the chaos doing what I'm doing. It makes sense if I'm fated to go through this life in a way that others can benefit from my difficulties. The corruption that pervades our society needs to stop – and not just in my life. This is the story of my journey through the darkness of deceit and corruption that exists in the State of Florida, which I hope can help bring some light to our world before it's too late.

This story is based on fact.
However, in our society, you can't tell the whole truth.
You have to disguise it so you don't get sued.
Hence names have been disguised or omitted to protect
the guilty.

Chapter I

Maximum Security

August 2007

I once went to a metaphysical church where I was overwhelmed by the positive energy. There was such a feeling of love and light that I felt joy just walking into the field. I am most struck as I walk through the nine gates of metal bars to my new assignment at this infamous State Prison by the dearth of that positive energy. The void is almost physically painful. The people around me seem to be bracing themselves as they walk in – as though they are holding their breath before jumping into icy cold water. I later come to know well why they've developed this posture. I notice as time passes, I'm doing the same thing. We are not prisoners, yet we feel imprisoned.

The journey to my office is a slow one. Each gate must close behind me before the one ahead can open. All I can think about is how long it would take to get out if there were a riot – or a fire. "High risk job" takes on new meaning at this prison; people earn their extra retirement here.

I'm met by the lead psychologist, Dr. Fielding, a tall, slender woman in her forties with pasty pale skin riddled with freckles, and wavy auburn hair tied back in a ponytail. She looks like she has been institutionalized for a long time herself. I had met her before at a workshop, and remember that she was rather quiet and reserved. She takes me on a tour of the prison. The main prison is a three-story building with cell blocks extending out of a long hallway running from one end of the prison to the other.

Dr. Fielding's office is in the basement, under the clinic at the east end of the building. I meet the four other psychologists who work here along the way to my office on the other end of the long prison hallway. The first is Dr. Latanya Coleman, a resident, who supervises all the group work. The prison system does not require that their psychologists (or medical doctors for that matter) be licensed. Dr. Coleman is married with no children, and happy to have a good paying residency. Farther down the hallway is Dr. Patti Finley, who started at State Prison as a case manager while completing her doctoral work. She did both her internship and residency at State Prison, and now functions as Dr. Fielding's assistant, but still has her own group of case managers to supervise as well. She is a pretty young woman with long, blond hair, who looks very young to me – like she should still be in school. I'm later told she was somewhat of a wild child when she first came to State Prison, having a succession of affairs with security officers. Security is very fond of her. Then there's Dr. Darlene Davis, a tall, thin, young woman with straight, black hair, who seems very stiff, moving like a large doll. She apparently slipped in the bathtub recently, and injured her neck. She is housed at the administrative offices, because until recently, she was Dr. Fielding's assistant. They had some sort of falling out, and she was replaced by Dr. Finley. She doesn't seem too happy. Dr. Michael Harmon, interestingly enough, is the only male psychologist in this men's prison. He's a handsome young man, a recent graduate who wears scrubs and looks like he belongs on one of those TV shows where all the doctors are handsome young men. He's the friendliest of the bunch, and in charge of the crisis unit. And last is Dr. Lena Sabine, an obese woman in her fifties, with tight blond curls and dark circles under her eyes. She has been assigned to teach me the ropes. Dr. Sabine is a contract worker, who appeared very anxious and spoke with a tremor in her voice. She has been promised a job at a Southern prison as soon as her agency can find someone to take her place at State Prison. She is hopeful because they have told her they have a new graduate interested in her position.

The State psychologists get a bonus for working at this dangerous prison, but contract psychologists still make about $20,000 per year more than the State psychologists. The State psychologists are all wondering how they can transfer over to a contract position. Dr. Fielding tells them the state won't allow it.

The psychologists all ask me whether I volunteered for this assignment or whether I was volunteered. I tell them I was volunteered. I had angered the warden at the reception center where I had worked for a year and a half, and was shipped to this U.S. equivalent of Siberia. I'm on temporary assignment so I don't get even the extra bonus the other state psychologists get for working at this worst of all State Prisons. No, I'm not happy to be here and will get out of here as soon as I possibly can, I tell them. I've already interviewed with Dr. Loemann at Central (another nearby prison) and have been told that as soon as they can hire someone else at State Prison, I'll be the first to leave. The other psychologists have all been here for two to three years. I find out soon that all of the women psychologists are also looking for jobs. The problem is, they can't be transferred to another State Prison until someone is hired to replace them. Of course, no one within the system will voluntarily take a job here.

As we leave the other psychologists and walk down the long hallway, Dr. Fielding gives me a lesson in inmate attire – all combinations of blue and orange. How appropriate – the colors of the local football team. I soon find out that in football season, many staff wear scrubs in the same colors, which can be confusing if you don't know who's who. Inmates dressed all in orange are general prison population workers, who are allowed to walk the hallways alone and may work in the clinic. They have lesser crimes, live in the work camp next door, and do not require maximum security supervision. Inmates in blue are confinement inmates. Inmates get placed in confinement due to the violent crimes that got them sentenced to prison or due to their violent behavior after arriving at prison. Those with stripes on their pants are at the highest level of confinement (CM-III), do not have to be cuffed when they leave their cells, and can also work – typically on the wings. The CM-I's and II's are more violent and have to be cuffed when they leave their cells. Death row inmates wear orange shirts and blue pants. They have two officers with them when they leave their cells. All together, these are the most violent people in the state – the mass murderers, rapists, gang kings, and hit men – people without conscience, who would not hesitate to add more people to their victim list if given half a chance.

The inmate orderlies here are called "runarounds." They supposedly behave themselves well enough to be trusted around the women mental health workers. There are no female security officers on the wings, because female officers are not allowed to strip search male prisoners. The male officers don't exactly enjoy strip searching these guys either, and don't like that Mental Health so frequently needs them brought out to interview.

I already know the colors of security – brown or white. Sergeants and below wear brown. Lieutenants and above wear white shirts with their brown pants and are hence referred to as "white shirts."

The stench of man-sweat waffles through even the Clorox the orderlies are using to clean the floors. The drab army-green walls must be infused with the odor. My office is off a hallway that runs between E wing and F wing parallel to the main hallway – a few doors down from Dr. Sabine's office. We typically access our offices through the E wing door, although there is also access from F wing. Two sets of keys are required to get on the wings. One lock opens only from the outside and one from the inside. We stand outside waiting for the correctional officer with the key. Each key officer has the job of opening the doors to four to six wings off the main hallway, and spends the day walking back and forth between the doors. When the key officer arrives, he hits the large key against the metal door handle to alert the officer inside to open his lock. Today, the door opens quickly. Both officers are available.

The man-stench gets stronger as we enter the humid, unair-conditioned wing. A long, three story hallway with confinement cells lies in front as we enter. To the right is the security desk at the entrance to our offices. The officers are sharing a pot of coffee – something that you never saw at my last prison assignment where the water was contaminated with lead.

The inmate showers are at the beginning of the hallway, visible to anyone who enters the wing. I'm told not to stand where I can be seen as many of the inmates will expose themselves whenever there's a woman near. With little to do, I'm told many inmates become sex addicts. I'm thinking there's no way I'd go near the shower anyway if anyone were in there. I really need to get out of here soon! My only relief is that I'm assigned here temporarily.

My office looks like a closet with windows on both sides that have been painted over – apparently some time ago as the ugly, institutional, dark tan paint is now peeling off. One window faces the group room and the other the interview room. The officer tells me that the windows are painted because if the inmates could see me in the office they would expose themselves to me. That new job just can't come soon enough! The old wooden desk is empty on the left side – just holes giving a reminder that it once had drawers. An old computer is sitting unplugged on the desk. Dr. Sabine tells me they've called the computer technician to fix it. I have only one chair in the office. It sinks in the middle and my feet don't reach the floor. The arms keep me from pulling in close enough to the desk to type. There's no phone. I laugh loudly as I'm told the last person given this office went out to lunch on his first day of work and never returned. I wonder how I rate this ugliest of all offices in the worst of all prisons.

Not that the other offices on my wing are much better. Dr. Sabine's office has a window to the hallway with bars running vertically and horizontally, giving her a crisscrossed view of the world outside E wing. Nowhere here do you forget where you are. There's no escape other than the door with two keys. I'm not feeling real safe here. Dr. Sabine attempts to give me back some feeling of control, telling me to make a list of things I need for Esther, Dr. Fielding's secretary. A phone tops the list. Of course, they soon tell me that the phones do not call out except to other state offices. Apparently Security once made $64,000 worth of personal phone calls one month and direct access was cut off. Consequently, you have to get an officer in the control room to get an outside line or go to your car on your lunch break to use your cell phone. Cell phones aren't allowed in prisons. Guards at the first gate check to make sure you're not bringing one in. I'm just starting to build a house and need to stay in touch with contractors. This is not making my life any easier, but I guess they knew this when they sent me to this prison.

I work on my list for Esther. I'm asking for a new chair even though Dr. Sabine tells me they are very scarce and security steals them if you leave your door open. I comment on the stench, hoping it does not always smell so bad. Dr. Sabine tells me the guards used tear gas earlier to subdue a paranoid inmate. It's the tear gas that smells like body odor. The smell's not usually this strong. Happy day! If nothing else, I won't have to deal with the odor on a daily basis.

I'm introduced to Dr. Sabine's staff of master's level case managers - or psychological specialists as they're called in prison. There's Mr. Kravatz, a large, Jamaican man in his 30's, who I'm told is always up to date on his paperwork and rarely makes an error. Ms. Portland is a 50-ish woman with very short hair, who has lupus and recently got out of the hospital. Mr. Richmond is a career prison employee, who has been dating the same woman for thirty years, but has never lived with her or married her because he does not want to leave his flock of parrots, and she is allergic to them. Ms. Willert has three young children and frequently misses work as one of them is always sick. Ms. Byron is close to retirement and counting the days, but she does only initial assessments and does not get behind. And last, but not least, is the young Ms. Malvert, who is notable for her affair with a high ranking security officer much older than herself. She's reported to take long lunch hours with the officer, but oddly enough, seems to be able to keep up with her paperwork. She has a daughter, who is chronically ill, causing her to also frequently miss work.

I meet security on the wing. The sergeant is an obese man of Irish descent, who tells me right away that he does not like mental health and thinks we should just go away. I discover that he finds many ways to let us know we're not welcome. He delays in opening the door so we can get on the wing or leave the wing, delays in pulling the inmates for us to see, and has his staff leave us alone with violent inmates, who are supposed to be supervised by security at all times.

His companions are a young black man and a middle aged white man from Ohio. They mumble a hello. I noted that they were drinking coffee and asked whether it was safe to drink the water. I told them that at my prior assignment, there was a notice on the bulletin board saying the water had unsafe levels of lead in it so no staff drank it. The sergeant laughed, and said that it was perfectly safe – to drink all I wanted to drink. There was no notice on a bulletin board here.

Due to the extensive documentation required by the current lawsuit alleging that mental health services were denied an inmate, most case managers are chronically behind on paperwork. Because strict time limits must be observed in completing inmate visits and doing the corresponding paperwork, when one worker is out, the supervisor and the other case managers must take up the slack, completing the absent worker's appointments as well as their own that day.

Dr. Sabine tells me that she has more absenteeism than any other supervisor and consequently, she has to spend much of her time doing case management work rather than supervisory work. She's glad I'm there to take over covering for her absent employees so she can focus on her job search. She can't take this place much longer.

I'm sent with a psychological specialist, Ralph Richmond, to observe rounds. Due to the lawsuit, the psychological specialists have to go to every cell on a weekly basis to check on each inmate and document the visit on the inmate's daily activity sheet. We go to a CM-1 wing first. CM-1 is the most restrictive close management classification with the most violent offenders. The inmates can work their way up to higher levels of close management with more privileges if they behave while in prison. Many never leave CM level-1.

The cells here remind me of Hannibal Lecter's cell in that Jodie Foster movie. They have a flap they can pass things through to the outside. Except these cell walls aren't plexi-glass like Hannibal Lecter's – they're steel. You can only see the inmate through the flap in the door and a small plexi-glass window with holes in it so you can speak with the inmate without opening the flap. Mr. Richmond tells me inmates have been holding their flaps hostage – refusing to close them. They poke people passing by with their homemade weapons or throw out urine at them. While I realize that people like to test you when you're new at a prison and I don't know how much of what I'm being told at this point is exaggerated, I step back against the railing at the far side of the walkway – away from the doors with flaps held hostage. We stop

7

at every door and Mr. Richmond announces that we're doing Mental Health rounds. He asks the inmates if they're doing OK. They inevitably say that they are fine. Mr. Richmond tells me this is not typical. He usually gets some talkative inmates that want to complain about something.

I'm told the confinement cells are relatively new in the State Prison system. It used to be the law of the jungle with these worst of all inmates constantly fighting each other for power and the correctional officers just observing, thinking that justice is come by naturally in prison. It was only in recent years that the worst of the worst were locked into individual cells and shackled when brought out. They tell me it only takes thirty seconds for an inmate who has found or made a sharp object to get out of his handcuffs. Because of this, inmates are stripped searched every time they leave the cell.

Prison workers are very formal and superficially polite. I knew this from my prior assignment. Mental health workers call me "Dr. Humphreys" even though I tell them they can call me "Janet." Security calls me "Mrs. Humphreys" even though I tell them that "Mrs. Humphreys" was my mother's name. They can call me Janet or Dr. Humphreys, but I'm not married and I'm not "Mrs." anyone. Even when I was married, I wasn't a Mrs.; I never changed my name to my husband's name. In spite of all this explanation, as at my prior assignment, Security continued to call me "Mrs." And as at my other assignment, I didn't waste my breath after the initial explanation. Maybe it's their general lack of education. Other than the mental health workers, few people working in prisons have much education beyond high school and their brief coursework to become certified as corrections officers. Even the wardens, who handle million dollar prison budgets, rarely have even a bachelor's degree. On the other hand, maybe security is just trying to be annoying. Corrections officers fairly uniformly seem to resent mental health.

Security, I'm told, resents Mental Health because they blame them for the new order. There are still many working at the prison who can remember the old ways, which they think worked better. They don't realize how little power Mental Health actually has in this system. It was the lawsuits inmates brought against the State which brought on the changes – Mental Health was just witness to some of the "natural justice."

Back at my office, I smell smoke and walk out to the officer's desk. There's an officer sitting in the closet smoking – as if that would take care of the smoke. State policy, of course, prohibits smoking. Dr. Sabine says that we're supposed to report anyone we see smoking to the warden and he'll come back immediately to check it out. I'm thinking there's no way I'm reporting the guys with the only key to get off this wing full of violent men. I tell the Sergeant that I'm allergic to smoke and ask him if he can have the guys smoke in the bathroom on the other side of the wing. He receives the request surprisingly well, saying that he'll see what he can do with the day shift, but the night shift smokes all night in the interview room next to my office and there's nothing he can do about that. Maybe I can get moved to another wing – a nonsmoking wing. Dr. Sabine tells me there's no such thing. We're actually one of the better wings as far as smoking goes.

I get a call from Dr. Loemann at Central saying that we need to meet for an interview. He said that when we met before, he didn't actually do a formal interview and he needs to do that before he can hire me. I need to get with personnel and fill out the State application for the job. I get the application filed and schedule an appointment to meet with him Wednesday. I email Dr. Fielding for permission to go.

When I get to the prison 30 minutes away at 3:30 pm, Dr. Loemann says he's tired and really doesn't feel like interviewing me. He asks if we can set up an appointment for next week. He says he doesn't have my application anyway. I volunteer that I brought a copy with me and take it out of my bag, determined to secure my future job. He quickly dismisses me, saying he doesn't want to see it. Instead, he wants to show me some forms he made up. I'm incredulous! Why did he make me come in here today? He then proceeds to tell me I must be aware that I have a "terrible" reputation in the Dept. of Corrections. He says I'm known to be confrontational with wardens and that his workers have heard of me and don't want to work under my supervision. I'm taken aback by this, and ask him what he heard from the crew I supervised at the reception center, where I had worked prior to my "temporary assignment." He replied, "Oh, they love you." However, he says other people don't and one person refused to take a job at Central if he had to work under me. I ask why he wants to hire me if I have such a bad reputation. He replies that he also has a bad reputation and that anyone in Mental Health worth anything at all acquires a bad reputation. However, he has learned to get along with security, and is actually invited to the weekly poker games held by the wardens in the area. However, because of my bad reputation, he would require me to work as a case manager initially and "prove my worth." He would want me to start training with the new case managers next week and learn "his system." This demotion does not appeal to me at all – and this was my one hope of escaping the worst of all prisons! Can he even do this legally? I can answer this myself. Rules that apply elsewhere don't apply to prisons.

Somehow, this worst of all supervisors suddenly seems worse than the worst of all prisons. I'm surprised by the intensity of my reaction; I cry all the way home. I call Dora, one of my former staff at the reception center where I used to work to try to ascertain who the person was who refused the job if he had to work under my supervision. She didn't know of anyone who had interviewed there.

Even after asking around, there was no one. I ask Fran, who worked at Central prior to transferring to the reception center if she knew of anyone at Central who would have a problem working with me. She called her former coworkers and no one had a problem with me. OK, maybe there isn't anyone. Was this staged so I wouldn't leave State Prison? Once assigned to State Prison, you can't get out – now confirmed personally.

Landing in Prison: The Reception Center

This might be a good time to digress and explain a little more about how I ended up in the prison system and how I came to have my "bad reputation." I had worked comfortably for about nine years in a private practice in South Florida doing social security evaluations and therapy when two hurricanes came my way, battering my world. I had minor damage to my single story home, but there was considerable damage to the homes around me. Some of the homes had large holes in their upper levels and the apartments down the street were so damaged they had to be evacuated. It looked like someone took a demolition crane and knocked holes in the buildings with one of those large metal balls. Almost a hundred trees were blown over in my development alone. We lost power with each hurricane in the heat of the summer. I was without power three days with the first hurricane and a week with the second. In South Florida stepping outside in the summer is akin to stepping into a sauna. Even the sun setting brings little relief. I learned that showering in cold water, uncomfortable as that was, would cool me off enough that I could sleep. The gas stations had sold out of gas with so many people leaving the area to escape the hurricanes and with those staying fueling up their generators. So although there were people distributing bottled water and ice, the lines were long and many people didn't have gas to go to the few distribution sites in the city. Sewage flooded the streets and spilled into many homes.

I wasn't alone in wanting to move. Lots of people started moving north after experiencing the uncomfortable after effects of two hurricanes in a row. I figured if I was going to sell my home, I better do it quickly as there were lots of homes suddenly on the market. My two closest friends had already moved away. Another had died shortly before the last hurricane. There wasn't a lot of reason to stay anymore. It was a good time to move on.

I started looking for jobs online and saw a number of jobs for psychologists in prisons in the northern part of the state. I knew another psychologist who had worked in a prison in South Florida. Although prison work had never appealed to me, she said she really enjoyed her job and the benefits were great so I decided to go ahead and apply. It would be nice to be able to retire someday.

December 2005

I got two interviews right away. The first interview was at the reception center, and did not really convince me that this was

11

where I would want to be. I met with Dr. Cramer, the psychologist consultant in the area and Dr. Williams, the medical director. I had already talked with Dr. Cramer by phone and had actually met him years before while we were both students at FSU. The formal interview was short – just the questions required by the state. They had been two years with an empty psychologist position and another psychologist on medical leave so I knew they would take anyone they could convince to interview. They took me on a tour of the prison, which reminded me of a college campus with buildings spread out over large, grassy areas. The inmates wore blue uniforms and walked freely around the compound. While Dr. Cramer seemed eager to have me there, I didn't feel I really connected with Dr. Williams, who would be my supervisor (but who I knew would hire me anyway). However, after being made to wait an hour for the subsequent interview at the women's prison with no apology, being subjected to inane questions, and then not so much as given a tour of the prison where I'd be working, the decision became much easier. In fact, the whole interview process was so outrageous that I wondered later if Dr. Cramer had been involved in discouraging me from taking the job at the women's prison.

In any case, I was excited about my new job. Having worked in the isolation of four walls for nine years in private practice, I was looking forward to the wide open spaces of the prison compound. I was also happy about having staff to work with after years of working on my own. And most importantly, there was the retirement. Working a high risk job, I was given double the normal state retirement. I'd actually be able to retire after ten or fifteen years. Doctors in private practice have no retirement. I'd been spending my extra money helping my daughter through college and there wasn't much left for a retirement account.

February 2006

The sign on the wall at the reception center entrance said "Security is not convenient." I was later told that this sign was put up after a medical intern assigned there complained of being

12

searched. After security searched my purse, I was directed to pass through the two gates to the prison. The two gates gave the feeling of being in a cage like an old time elevator with a barred door on the front and the back. As at the state prison, only one door of the cage could open at a time to prevent an inmate from running through. I stepped between the gates with several other people on this elevator to nowhere. I wasn't crazy about this feeling of confinement and was relieved when the door on the other side opened to the green.

I was greeted by another psychologist, Dr. Torvin. He didn't share my excitement about working for the prison system. He had a conflict with Dr. Cramer while at another prison, and was sent back to the reception center. It was obvious he was not happy to be back. He had never been happy working for the prison system, and had left on a couple of occasions to go into private practice. I wouldn't let him disillusion me. He seemed very bitter.

Dr. Torvin took me on another tour of the prison, and I was happy to get the lay of the land one more time. Inmates walked freely between buildings separated by large green spaces, slept in open dorms, and were not apparently considered any great danger to staff.

I was assigned to supervise the intake unit, which was housed under the juvenile dorm. Following conviction, inmates in the north part of the state were filtered through the reception center where they were assigned to their regular prison after medical and psychological screenings. When we arrived at the intake building, I was greeted by Jake, the psych. specialist who acted as supervisor for the two years my position was vacant. I remember asking at the interview how Jake would feel having to leave the supervisory position after two years. Dr. Williams said he'd probably be happy to get out from under the paper work and get back to seeing inmates. Jake was pleasant, but reserved. I wondered how he really felt about being replaced. It was not long before I found out.

My office was a pleasant surprise. I had a large room with windows across one side looking out on a green. There was a large, L-shaped desk, two file cabinets, and a book case. I could live with this.

Jake took me around to meet the staff and Lenora, our security guard. Lenora was a pleasant young woman, who just got her realty license and hoped to soon leave her day job. Unfortunately for us, she soon was able to do so.

I had a staff of six psychological specialists. I looked to Jake to provide me with a job description of some type. Jake told me there was no manual outlining my job duties or the workings of the intake process. He said that everyone did their job their own way and it worked out. He just had a problem with some people's writing skills. He was an English major and was outraged by their destruction of the English language. He said he would help me learn my job, but he was not happy about it. He told me flat out that he enjoyed being supervisor and that he resented being replaced. He especially resented that he was not given advance notice. I was just dropped on him. He did not seem to recognize that he did not have the background for the position. He felt that his years working in prison were all the experience he needed to do the job.

I found that as Jake said, everyone had their own interpretation of what was to be done. They were proud that they could evaluate the inmates arriving at the reception center in ten minutes or less to determine whether they needed mental health care. In fact, they competed every month for a Mardi Gras necklace – a prize Jake gave the psych. specialist who completed the most intake screenings. Quality was not an issue; the warden demanded quantity and they were good at meeting those demands.

Some of the psych. specialists had been with the intake unit for several years. They were confident they knew the best way to do their job. One of the women told me the Intake Unit ran itself like a "smooth machine," and they actually had no need for a supervisor. I told her I'd try not to get in the way of their "smooth" running, but she asked me every day for weeks why I came back to work there. Didn't I know they didn't want me there? I later found out they had placed bets on how long it would take them to get rid of me. The most popular bet was three months. How was it that these people were so bold? Is this what comes from extreme job security?

They told me about their supervisor six years ago, who stayed late all the time so he could collect overtime. There was no actual work to do after the inmates were sent back to their dorms for count at 4:00. He spent his time writing reports for the private practice he kept on the side. They had another supervisor for about six months two years before I got there. She did no work at all - just sat in the office all day keeping books for her husband's business. They didn't appreciate that. Did I intend to do some work?

One of the women, Dora, who seemed to actually want to be of help to me, showed me a recent posting on the bulletin board, which advised staff that recent testing showed that the prison water had elevated levels of lead. Staff did not drink the water. I should bring water from home. I wondered what they did about the inmates' water. Nothing, I was told. They drink the lead.

My clerk, Rene, let me know right off that she had lived in the county all her life and that she knew everyone at this prison. Her grandfather had worked here, her mother and her aunt worked here, and she was good friends with the warden, who lived down the street from her. It seems families have lived in this part of the state for generations and consider the prisons the family business. There's little other industry in these parts.

Rene was also friends with the local sheriff and knew all the deputies. She told me that people in this county don't like outsiders. I should cut my losses and leave early rather than later. She did very well for two years without supervision and did not feel she needed a supervisor now.

Well, I wanted a new challenge – but this big a challenge? I told myself it takes time for people to adjust to change.

Meanwhile, I wondered why I'd been dropped in the intake unit without hearing from my supervisor. In fact, it was three days before I got a call inviting me to his office. By this time, I had a lot to tell him and a lot to ask him.

Dr. Carlos Williams' office was on the second floor of the medical building. Dr. Williams was a tall, dignified man, who traveled an hour and a half to get to work every day. He liked the community where he lived and said he did not mind the commute. He still had much more time with his family than when he was in

15

private practice. He liked working in a prison where so many rare diseases show up – more than he ever saw in private practice. Finally someone who was happy with his job! Dr. Williams was a medical doctor, who knew little of the psychology intake process. He did know it wasn't working at all well. In fact, he told me the intake department was his "worst nightmare." He knew that staff came in very late and left very early. He didn't think anyone over there did much. He wanted me to tighten things up. He knew of no guidelines or written procedures for the operation of the department either. I had to make it up as I went along.

I sat in on intake screenings with each of the psych. specialists to learn the system. Our job here was to screen inmates for mental illness when they came into the prison system, and make appropriate referrals to psychiatrists or counselors. That much everyone agreed on. On their first day at the reception center, inmates went through the receiving department, and were checked out by a nurse. Someone from our unit went over to give a brief talk about the mental health services available to the inmates. On the second day, inmates received a group video orientation, following which we administered a group IQ test and a one page depression screening. Anyone who scored high on the depression inventory would be seen immediately following the testing to screen for suicide risk. On the third day, the inmates saw a doctor for a physical. On the fourth day, they saw a classification worker for assignment to their permanent prison, and then came to us for a mental health screening in whatever time was left. Why they went to classification before coming to mental health did not make a lot of sense since the classification would have to be changed if they required mental health care. In any case the warden wanted the inmates moved out to the West Unit after the fourth day to make room for the next shipment of inmates. However, medical couldn't process 100 inmates in one day and often went into the 4th or 5th day. However, because mental health was the last to see the inmates, on paper it showed that we were the ones who were behind.

It seems there really was no uniform way of doing the mental health interview and no one had ever written down procedures for the intake process. The psych. specialists just filled in blanks on a computer screen on a very frustrating program developed before there was a concept of "user friendly." Every page had its own set of prompts, which was different from the page before. I had to go by what staff told me, and each one told me something different. They all had different opinions on what they were supposed to write on each of those computer screens.

As I sat in with each psych specialist and discussed their decisions as to whether to refer their inmate for psychiatric treatment, I realized how little they knew about diagnosing mental illness. Most of them came to their prison jobs straight from graduate school with no real training in psychological assessment. Only one was actually licensed as a mental health counselor. Several said they always considered anyone with depression to have an "adjustment disorder" since they must be adjusting to prison. An intake usually took them between five and ten minutes. They sometimes had 100 people to screen in one day, and they had to be fast. Yet somehow, they usually had time left to nap, read a novel, or leave early. My work was cut out for me.

I eventually got a call from the assistant mental health director at the State Capital. Dr. Zircon welcomed me to my job, but then lectured me on how mental health in prisons is very different than in private practice and I really shouldn't try to apply what I learned outside to my prison job. He told me that what I should be doing is actually triage and it shouldn't take long. I'm confused, .because triage is used to determine in what order people need to be seen. Triage is in no way sufficient to determine whether someone needs mental health treatment. Apparently, the workers here were just trained in doing triage. How scary is that? Many of the inmates passing through were imprisoned for violent crimes, most likely caused by impulse control problems related to their mental illness. You don't need to be a psychologist to know that violent people probably have some mental issues. If they are not diagnosed in prison, the cycle will not stop and they'll probably be back on the streets preying on others. There are reasons for the high rate of recidivism, and this has got to be a major one.

I called my regional consultant, Dr. Cramer, to see if he had any guidelines for the operation of the intake unit. He did not. He suggested I phone other intake units around the state for guidance.

17

One intake supervisor was a psychology resident. She complained she had not been given the supervision she was promised so that she could get licensed. She was at a much smaller prison where they see about a third of the inmates we see, but she had an extra person scoring the tests. She had her psych specialists doing a full assessment on each inmate, which can take an hour or more if the inmate has any problems. I called another intake supervisor, who had been on the job for ten years. He saw about the same number of inmates as we did, but had more workers. His workers did a full assessment as well, which took about forty-five minutes. I was glad to see nobody else was just doing triage.

I resolved to teach my staff to do full assessments. Unfortunately, they resolved to resist. What they had been doing had been good enough for years and they didn't see why they should do anything different. I gave a workshop on how to do an assessment, and gave handouts with a list of questions to ask. I invited them to watch me as I did an intake assessment. Oddly enough, they complied with sitting in on assessments with me. Curiosity must have got the better of them. However, they didn't want to implement the new system themselves. They acted as if I had made up this whole thing to torment them. I let them know that this was the international format for assessments and that we needed to do an adequate assessment to get the inmates the help they needed and also to better protect society. They said no one cared about that here – the warden just wanted to get the inmates out as quickly as possible. I told them it was a matter of ethics. I asked them to bring any cases they were referring for further treatment to me for supervision. They complained I was micromanaging them.

I got a three-ring binder and started creating a policy and procedures manual. As unresolved issues came up, I took them to staff meeting and together we created the procedures. I wrote them down, copied everyone, and left the procedures notebook on the bookcase in the hall where everyone had access to it.

Jake was becoming increasingly hostile, and was taking more and more time off. Two other staff took frequent leave without pay as they had no sick leave left. This left us half-staffed much of the time, so we struggled to keep up with the work.

Meantime, Rene, the clerk, came in late every day. We relied upon her to get our charts from the medical records room and couldn't start our work in the mornings until the charts came in. Dora fortunately volunteered to pick up our charts on her way in each morning. She drove over an hour to work and always came in early. When Dora injured her back, I started getting the charts.

I ended up writing up Rene on three occasions, but Dr. Williams cautioned me not to file anything formally against her as her family was very powerful. In the end, the file I kept with her complaints disappeared from my file cabinet.

July 2006:

Time flies and nothing seemed to change. In staff meetings the same complaints came up about things not being like they were in the good old days – before I appeared. My staff actually complained about having to take a lunch hour. People who complain about having to take a lunch hour must have been too long with the State. "On the streets" as inmates called the outside world, people would be happy to have a lunch hour. I worked through my lunch frequently in private practice – through my lunch, through my evenings, and through my weekends. Then one of my staff, an unlicensed social worker, complained about the indignity of not being allowed to make clinical decisions. He was demoralized because he was being "micro-managed." Unlicensed people, of course, could not have worked for two years without supervision "on the streets." Only in a state prison are unlicensed psych specialists allowed the autonomy they had prior to my appearance. Yet none of this moved them. I spoiled their fun and they weren't going to let me forget it so easily.

About half my staff (those who resisted change the most) attended weekly "prayer meetings" at lunch. It seemed strange that Jake attended these meetings since he early on declared himself an atheist. I wondered what these meetings were really about.

I found out early on that a sort of primitive Christian religion is prominent in this backward area of the country. Our new security officer read her Bible as she screamed profanities at the inmates in our waiting room. My clerk kept her *Daily Bread* readings in her desk for easy reference. Their god is a harsh, punitive god and the prison system mirrors the punitive and controlling nature of their god-fearing religion. Somehow no one seems to see any of this as incongruous with Jesus' teachings. Religion and prison punishment seem to perfectly complement and feed each other in this environment.

I noticed that the women working in the prison had to get their husbands' permission to do whatever they wanted to do as if this were a perfectly normal thing to do. What happened here? It's like women's lib totally missed this area sixty years ago. I'm thinking I've been transported back in time. This prison is in the Bible belt, but I guess I never before realized what that meant even though I've lived in this State for over twenty years.

Security quizzed me about my religious background and whether I went to a "Bible-based church." My clerk was appalled that I believed in evolution and declared that "Christians" don't believe in evolution – only creationism. I was a heretic apparently. I didn't believe in a literal interpretation of the Bible.

I eventually had to transfer Jake to another unit as he openly refused to change the way he did assessments and declared in a staff meeting that he was "never" going to do things my way. Another one of my frequently absent specialists left for another job, and the difficult clerk got herself transferred out and promoted (for giving me a hard time?). So I was able to hire new staff who were more amenable to doing what I required. After doing things "my way" for a while, the old staff who stayed on, seemed to get the merit of doing an actual assessment. It became a pleasant work environment with staff motivated to help the inmates.

However, the outpatient unit was being flooded with new inmates that were actually being diagnosed with mental illnesses that required counseling and psychiatric treatment, and Dr. Torvin was getting upset that we were creating extra work for him. He started appearing in the parking lot when I was leaving and screamed at me that I needed to go back to the "old way" of doing things. After I told Dr. Williams that I felt I was being stalked, Dr. Torvin quit his open attack on me. Dr. Torvin also went to the weekly "prayer meetings" that seemed to be anything but prayer meetings. When Dr. Williams asked him to send one of his staff over to help us out when I had several people sick, he delayed in doing so. It was often several days later when one of his crew showed up, saying they could only work for a few hours. One of his staff was housed part-time in our building, and I could see him reading novels while we scurried to see inmates. Dr. Torvin's crew didn't seem to have all that much to do.

At this prison, the "runarounds" were called "permanents" as these were inmates assigned to the reception center as their permanent placement after screening. They were given jobs helping out staff or cleaning the grounds. Our permanent, Daniels, put labels on files, photocopied, and kept inventory of our testing supplies. He was good at his job.

Dora showed me how to look up inmates' charges. Daniels was a nonviolent sex offender; he had sex with a fifteen year old. Dora told me that most of the permanent inmates working at the reception center have charges similar to Daniels and are at low risk for violent behavior. They can walk freely around the compound.

Daniels gave me his complaints about the corrections system in Florida. He, like many others, came to Florida on vacation, and will leave on probation. Unlike many inmates, he acknowledged that he did wrong. His main complaint was not about his own punishment, but about people being put in prison for not paying their debts. He pointed out that our ancestors came to this country to escape debtor's prisons and yet we have created the same system here. People are serving prison terms for not paying child support or even for not paying traffic tickets.

We receive a full range of inmates from minimum to maximum security at the reception center - everybody but the death row inmates - who are taken directly to the maximum security prison as it would be too dangerous to bring them here. At intake, we assign, inmates "S codes." S1 inmates do not require mental health treatment and can go to a regular camp. S2 inmates either require counseling (but not medication) or score below a 76 on IQ testing and are felt to be too low functioning to get along in a regular camp. Finally, S3 inmates are those with psychiatric problems severe enough to require medication and are sent to what are known as "psych camps." These psych camps have a

21

reputation of being violent places, and some inmates will lie about their psychiatric problems or refuse medication so they won't have to go to a psych camp.

If inmates scored below a 76 on their BETA group IQ test, we had to confirm this low score with an abbreviated individual IQ test called the WASI. If they scored low again on the WASI, we had to administer a full-length individual IQ test called the WAIS, which can take over an hour. This is far too much time spent with one inmate when we have so many to see. Inmates can sign a refusal for the testing if they agree to being assigned to an S2 camp. We hope for refusals as all this testing just gets us further behind. Even if an inmate has been here before and already had the three IQ tests, we're required to do it again. I sent an email to the DOC Secretary's suggestion box, suggesting that even Social Security does not require repeat IQ testing after the age of 18 to qualify for disability. The scores are pretty stable after that age. DOC could save a lot of money and our time if we did not require repeat testing. No response to that.

The worker who did an inmate's suicide profile after testing would see that same inmate for the intake screening. I did a suicide profile on a very irritable repeat offender named Kelly so I had the good fortune of seeing him again for intake. He got a 74 on his Beta IQ test – just three points below where he needed to be to go to an S1 camp. I silently groaned. Not only did I have to screen this irritable person, already angry he had to take the first test, but I also had to give him a follow-up IQ test to confirm his low score. Security told me he was being a pain in the waiting room. I called his name and followed him back to the office. We are told to always walk behind the inmates. I announced nonchalantly as we enter the office, that we would be starting with a "vocabulary exercise" – my theory being that if I don't say the word "test," he won't notice I'm actually giving him a test. He doesn't fall for it. He knows the system better than I do. The letter in front of his DC number is a "K." He's been here twelve times. He wants to sign a refusal. I give him the refusal form. He signs and gets up to leave. I tell him we have to finish the rest of the interview, promising to make it quick. The angry inmate answers every question with "Don't know." I suggest he might like some medication to help with his irritability and impatience. He says he likes being irritable. In fact, he likes being able to explode and scare other people. He feels good after he explodes. He says he's already killed two people and doesn't care about how he affects anyone else. Other people need to worry about how they affect him. I quickly run through the required questions. He says he just wants to be an S1 – he doesn't need any help.

I explained to him that because he chose not to take the WASI test, I had to make him an S2 and he would go to a camp with counseling available. He laughed and said he didn't care. He said he would rule any camp he went to. He just didn't want to have to take the test. He told me the problem with men these days is that they aren't men anymore and women have had to take over. He said he's a man and he's in charge. I wish him well and escort him out.

Then there was the gang leader with Bipolar Disorder. He had been in Federal Prison for six years, but had always refused treatment. He said he always stayed in trouble in prison because of his impulse control problem, but needed to stay alert and didn't want to take medication. He only had a year to go in state prison and was fearful of getting in trouble once he got out. He didn't want to go to back to gang life.

Most of the inmates we saw were not violent, and most people would be surprised by what brought them to prison. I saw an inmate with an IQ of 65, categorizing him as mentally retarded. He was in for repeat violations – unpaid traffic tickets. Is this the purpose of prison? Do we need protection from these people who don't pay their traffic tickets? This inmate had worked all his life – had never asked for public assistance despite his low IQ. He didn't know where to go to pay the fines. He always paid his bills in cash. He said he got his job in a high school work program, and stayed with the same company to work since. Will he be able to get his job back when he gets out? Would he know how to get another job? Or will he be joining the public assistance rolls, applying for disability when he gets out?

We once had an eighty year old man with no prior arrests, who was imprisoned for failing to pay traffic tickets. He couldn't afford both food and traffic fines so he opted for food. Is this really someone we need protection from?

January 2007

I see many more inmates sent to prison for absurdities. One violated his probation by attending his father's funeral and not making it back before curfew. Another was playing his music too loudly. Both got a year and a day in prison for their violations. Then there were the inmates who did not pay their child support. How exactly are they going to pay their child support in prison? They're ripped away from their children, traumatizing them as well. Then the State (us taxpayers) will likely have to support not only Dad in prison (at the tune of almost $18,000/year), but the kids as well through AFDC, food stamps, and maybe even housing programs. When they get out, the Dads will have a prison record and won't have a driver's license, making it more than a little difficult to find work, and making it more likely that they'll be returning to prison again for nonpayment of child support. What happened to the heart of America? How can we do this to families?

Security laughed when I complained about these people being sent to prison for ridiculous reasons. They like the laws requiring imprisonment for any violation of probation. It keeps things black and white and guarantees their job security. The whole idea of the purpose of prisons being to protect the public seems to have gotten lost somewhere. Now we enact laws to preserve the prison workers' jobs – or perhaps more likely, to protect the income of the wealthy prison contractors.

There were also inmates who voluntarily came back to prison. Some could not find jobs with their prison records and were tired of being hungry and living on the streets. Others without health insurance committed a crime they knew would get them enough time to get whatever treatment they required.

July 2007

I spent a year training the psych. specialists in mental disorders and teaching them (largely against their will) to conduct a proper initial assessment which could take up to an hour. This upset the warden, who wanted us to be able to process up to one hundred inmates within four hours so she could stay on schedule. I told her that ethically I could not do what had been done there in the past. I had inmates who had been admitted seven or eight times and had never been diagnosed or treated for the Bipolar Disorder or other severe mental disorders that kept getting them in trouble. *But then treating them might slow down the revolving door that keeps these prisons in business. I was aware of this even then.*

We were housed in an old, two story building. The juveniles who were sentenced to adult prison were housed above us. Staff pointed out one day that sewage was raining on our files in the hallway. They told me that the juveniles like to stuff their toilets and they overflow on us. This time apparently the juveniles were upset that our security officer had badgered an intellectually challenged inmate. Flooding us with sewage was their way of complaining. The dental department moved out of this building as it was unsanitary, but it was deemed OK for mental health staff.

The warden at the reception center tried to make me uncomfortable enough to leave the reception center on my own. We had an old air conditioner in our building and it froze up in the heat of the summer so we had no air conditioning when we needed it the most. Most of my staff had fans, but I was told my first summer there that no new fans could be brought into the prison - only those "grandfathered in" could stay. I went home every day with a headache from working in the Florida heat. I offered to donate a window air conditioner to help the existing unit handle the heavy load, but was told that would be impossible. No explanation, of course, was given as to why it would be impossible to make a donation to the State. One of my staff eventually complained to the union about the lack of air conditioning as well as the mold and mildew on the carpet due to the damp conditions.

The warden, interestingly enough, wanted me to back her up and say there was no problem with the air conditioning. She became enraged when I would not.

Long before this last confrontation with the warden, our security officer began sending away inmates that we needed to see, making us even more behind. Medical records hid the charts we needed. The classification unit, who saw the inmates before we did, kept the inmates longer so we had less time to process them. The warden sent inmates to the unit next door before we saw them so I had to spend much of my time working with lists, and checking the computer to see where the inmates were housed so I could send for them.

During all this time, Dr. Cramer's comment was that "this house belongs to security and we are just visitors." I would have to get along. Although he was housed at the front of the prison, he never came back to see what was going on or help out in any way. He suggested I call the psychologist at the other reception center to see if he had any suggestions. The psychologist at the other reception center told me he had a waiting room which held 100 inmates and he didn't have to do call-outs. The inmates were brought in as a group so he got to see them all at once. There was no one sending them off to a West Unit before he could see them. He said he couldn't function under the conditions at my prison. He actually had a day off in the middle of the week when his reception center sent about a hundred of their inmates to our prison for screening. How does this make sense? We're overloaded, working under impossible conditions, and they get a day off? Someone later told me this occurred as a result of a poker game between the wardens of our two prisons. I summarized our conversation in an email to Dr. Cramer, and copied Dr. Williams and the hospital administrator. This information was not well received. Rather than providing a larger waiting room or reorganizing to make our task feasible, the hospital administrator advised me that I would never again talk to or email anyone outside of this prison –or else!

I was called by the nurse to get another TB test. This was my 3rd in the past year. Sometimes my whole unit was called in for testing. The nurse said that only Dora and I had to report for testing this time. It's not unusual for inmates to come in with TB.

I asked the nurse who we were exposed to this time, but she did not know. It had been some time since I had gone to the testing room, and I had been seeing few inmates as most of my time was being spent juggling lists of inmates being sent to the West Unit without my knowledge and trying to get them back for their evaluations. I couldn't think of anyone that both Dora and I would have seen. I told the nurse I wouldn't be coming in for another test if she couldn't tell me who I was exposed to. She said I needn't bother coming in to work on Monday if I didn't get tested before then. So I got one more test for no apparent reason.

Security transferred our competent "permanent" inmate to another job, and we had a number of less than competent permanents (one did not know the alphabet and could not alphabetize our files for us) before we finally got someone who could do the job. One day, our new, competent, permanent told me he was being accused of having an "inappropriate" relationship with me. Security said he had been spying on our security officer for me and had met with me that morning to tell on her. Since I hadn't spoken to him at all that morning, I could honestly say this was not true. I went to the lieutenant to complain. This permanent was the first competent person we had been assigned in months and we wanted to keep him. The lieutenant denied that the permanent was being moved due to anything inappropriate going on. He said it was just his time to be rotated. The lieutenant said he did find it curious, however, that I took such an interest in him, and suggested that maybe "something" was going on between us.

Oddly enough, the next morning my supervisor, Dr. Williams, told me that security had told him I was inappropriate with the permanent, confiding in him problems I was having with staff. I told him security needed to get their stories straight since the story I had heard was that the permanent was inappropriately telling me what our security guard was doing. In any case, I guess they couldn't allow our permanent to stay when they saw his loyalty was to mental health and not to security. They were right, of course. He had actually been letting me know when security was sending away people we needed to see. The next permanent we were assigned could barely read and could not in any way keep up with the workload we had for him. He could typically be seen standing outside the bathroom door anytime a woman was inside. Eventually, a female security guard got tired of seeing him lurking there and got him transferred out.

I was allowed to bring in a fan my second summer at the reception center when a new hospital administrator was hired. However, I was still told I could not donate an air conditioner and the harassment stepped up. One rainy day, I came into my office and found that the cord on my fan had been stripped, and the fan had been plugged in with the cord stretching across the floor under my desk. I called the Major to report the incident, and he told me not to file a written incident report. He would send me some electrical tape and I could repair my cord. My staff were appalled that what one of them called a "murder attempt" was being swept under the rug. I took the cord to Dr. Williams anyway. Someone had to be made aware of what was going on.

My clerk joined in the sabotage, failing to order testing supplies and failing to send "call-outs" for the inmates we hadn't yet seen. She blamed her forgetfulness on her divorce although she already had someone else lined up to marry. Is it a sin in this primitive religion to be a divorced woman even if her husband left her for someone else? Does a woman lose status without a man? Is it OK to divorce if you remarry quickly and cancel out the bad act of divorce? I have to reference my childhood fifty some years ago to see if this makes sense in their world view. Yes, we had a divorced neighbor when I was a child, and my mother didn't want me to hang out with her or her daughter. I did anyway. She was a teacher and told me at the age of five that I was precocious. I liked her. They ended up moving to a city where they wouldn't be ostracized as they were in our small Ohio town.

Difficult as it was working in this environment that felt more and more like summer camp with me being the targeted kid and the brunt of a million not so nice pranks, I liked my work and was determined to stick it out. I felt like I was making a difference for the prisoners coming in. And besides being able to feel I had some purpose in this ridiculous system, I wanted the double retirement that would allow me to retire someday. I finally had workers trained to do their job when I received notice that I was being "temporarily assigned" against my will to the "death row" prison.

Since I wouldn't cave in to their bullying and leave on my own, they found a way to step up my punishment.

Days before leaving for my new assignment, one of my workers approached me distraught, telling me people were saying "horrible things" about me. She was too uncomfortable apparently to tell me what these "horrible things" were, but another worker, overhearing the conversation, shouted out, "They're saying you're not a 'real' Christian!" Not a real Christian? Maybe I am that divorced teacher back in the fifties!

August 2007

Back at the death row prison, Dr. Sabine came in very upset. Apparently, the private company she contracts with was advertising the job they were supposed to be holding for her in the Southern part of the State. She wouldn't be allowed to leave either. They weren't able to find anyone to take her place at State Prison. She tells me the story of a woman who was hired at State Prison, but seeing all the barbed wire and hearing the inmates shouting from the parking lot, drove off without ever entering the nine gates. Dr. Sabine seemed to be getting more and more anxious. The circles under her eyes seem deeper. She is revving up her job search. She'll look for something outside the prison system, even if it pays less.

We occasionally get locked out of our offices if F wing has to open their door to our offices. The E and F wing doors can't both be opened at once or inmates could run through from one wing to another (if anyone was out of his cell). I don't ask why the door is locked anymore – just how long it's going to be. If it will be long, I can go to F wing and wait for the key people to let me in through that wing. I'm told it shouldn't be more than a few minutes so I decide to wait it out. I can write up my last contact while I wait. "Hurry up and wait" is the motto here. We do more waiting than anything else.

The "runaround" orderly has the lunch cart. The officers go downstairs to talk to a noisy inmate. I don't pay attention to the inmate as I write. However, when I look up, the inmate jumps back behind the food cart. I ask him what he's doing in a strong voice. I can see through the metal bars of the cart that his pants are undone. I tell him to step out beside the cart. He arranges his pants and complies. I tell him to stand where I can see him and keep his hands on the cart. He stands there uneasily for a few minutes and then says he's going to see what's going on downstairs and runs downstairs to join the officers. I wonder if this is some kind of initiation hazing. Why would he run to the officers if he thought they would discipline him for this behavior? I decide not to let the officers know I'm upset. I talk to Ms. Portland, who has been "gunned" many times. (In prison, an inmate's exposing himself is referred to as "gunning.") Ms. Portland is very angry that this frequent "gunning" goes on.

I wonder why it is that so many inmates "gun" the women on a regular basis. I worked for a year and a half at the reception center and none of my staff were flashed during that time. One guy grabbed his crotch during an interview with one of the women, but that was the worst that ever happened. Why is it that these same inmates, when they come to State Prison, flash the women on a daily basis? Seems like security could handle it here too if they wanted to. I decide right then that I will transfer any inmate that guns a female case manager to a male case manager so that they learn they will lose all contact with women if they act out. Why hasn't this been done before?

We could smell smoke in our offices. The loud, screeching alarm was sounding. There was a fire on a wing down the hall. I go out to the quarterdeck to ask the Sergeant what was happening. He said a death row inmate on G wing had set his mattress on fire. I tell him I'll be evacuating now. He tells me I need to go back to my office as we're "locking down." Wait a minute. This is a fire – there's got to be an evacuation plan, right? Actually no – any emergency results in "lock down." All inmates go back to their cells and no one can either come off or on the wing. Security has the only key out. The officer tells me they're not allowed to leave the inmates no matter what happens – and neither are we. How does this make sense? If something went wrong, wouldn't a bunch of women, untrained to handle violent inmates, present more of a liability on the wing than a help? What kind of idiotic policy is this?

I go back to my office and lock my door to wait it out. Shortly after the wing opens up again, I get a call asking if I know where Mr. Kravatz is. He has the chart of the inmate who set fire to his mattress and they need it in medical. I start calling the other wings, looking for Mr. Kravatz. I'm told they're evacuating the building and I need to get out. I wonder why we weren't advised of this on our wing. The psych. specialist who answered the phone said she was just told by a "white shirt" that we needed to go to the visiting park. I check with our wing Sergeant – he knows nothing about it. I tell him I'm going to check it out. I check my other staff offices on the wing to advise them to evacuate, but no one else was on the wing. As I go out, I'm warned to watch my step because the inmate who set his cot on fire bled all over the hallway. I pass two white shirts on my way out who say they don't know what's happening, but we need to evacuate. How interesting – a situation where we actually evacuate! What could that be? Then I meet some psych. specs in the hallway who say they went to the visiting park, but were sent back to their offices. They were told that only officers were to meet in the visiting park. I decide to check it out myself and walk through eight of the nine gates to the large room near the prison entrance where the inmates receive their visitors. I'm told that the meeting is only for officers and that I should go back to my wing. I'm not going back to the wing where I can be locked in if something happens!

I decide to wait it out in the Old Laundry Room, where a birthday party for all the August birthdays is soon in progress. My birthday is in August, but did not appear on the email with the other August birthdays.

There are only two office spaces that are not on wings with inmates – the Mental Health Administration offices where Dr. Fielding resides and the Old Laundry Room, which now houses a group of psych. specialists and the crisis unit. Because these offices are not on wings with the inmates, they don't have doors which lock on both sides, and can be easily accessed and exited. Consequently, these are highly prized office spaces. The psychologists strategize a plan to gain the Old Laundry Room office space for ourselves. We could all be housed together and support each other. It only makes sense that the workers should have immediate access to their supervisors in crisis situations. It wouldn't hurt to present this idea to Dr. Fielding.

The Old Laundry Room is packed with Mental Health workers. People are speculating there may be a bomb threat. Dr. Sabine says the Sergeant on E wing told her that he heard something about a gang war being planned on B wing. I'm wondering if anybody at this prison actually knows what's going on. Nobody in mental health wants to go back to the wings where they'll be locked in if anything happens. We hang out at the Old Laundry Room until it's time to go home. As we're leaving, officers from other prisons are arriving as backup. I'm just relieved that I'll get to miss whatever's going to happen.

The next morning, all is calm. Nothing unusual apparently happened the night before. I'm called to medical to translate for one of the psychiatrists. The inmate who set the fire does not speak English, and since I'm the only mental health worker who speaks Spanish, I get the job. I talk with security while I wait for the psychiatrist on duty, Dr. Steinberg, to finish up with another patient. They're very upset with the inmate who set the fire, because he stuffed his blanket in the toilet. When they went into his clinic cell to fix the toilet, they found he had stored up seven plastic cups full of his own excrement.

When I see the death row inmate, Cabrera, he tells me he hears the voice of a friend, Joey, who hung himself. His deceased friend told him that he needs to kill himself before security kills him. The inmate thought that security was planning to take him out to the recreation area so that the other inmates could have a "party" and kill him. He said the other inmates were telling stories about him that were not true. They said he had sex with animals and children. I asked him why he had stored the "poop" in his clinic cell. He said that he was saving it to protect himself from security. He had overheard them saying his name, and although he could not understand what they said since he spoke no English, he believed they were plotting to kill him. Dr. Steinberg tells Cabrera that he is in charge here and that he will not allow anyone to kill him. Dr. Steinberg comments on how much energy it takes to hold together delusions. I'm thinking maybe the friend's ghost may actually be causing him problems (I've read John Edwards'

32

books). I ask the inmate if he thinks his friend, Joey, might be lying to him to get him to join him on the other side. He smiles and acknowledges that his deceased friend is capable of lying.

There are two other psychiatrists at State Prison, who I am soon to meet. One is a harsh, Polish man, Dr. Helmut Pierkosky, who has little regard for American psychiatry. He lets everyone know that he is the only well-trained psychiatrist with the State because he was trained in Europe. The other psychiatrist is Dr. Ann Chu, a diminutive Chinese woman, who lets me know right away that she hates working at this prison and is transferring out as soon as possible. She complains that both Dr. Steinberg and Dr. Pierkosky give the inmates too much Vistaril so they can sleep away their days. Did I know that Dr. Steinberg lost his medical license for overprescribing pain killers? That's why he's here. He can't get his license back, but he can work at a prison without a license, and he's still overmedicating.

I'm asked to come in early while the death row inmate is in the infirmary so I can translate for Dr. Steinberg. They've applied to have Inmate Cabrera transferred to the Crisis Stabilization Unit (CSU) at a neighboring prison, but all the beds are taken at the moment. The inmate did not get his medication for the first few days. Dr. Steinberg said that nothing happens when the head nurse is out. There's no point in complaining – she'll be back in a day or two. It's a little disconcerting that the failures of the prison healthcare system are so easily accepted; the doctor must feel powerless here too. Inmate Cabrera tells his story over the next few days. He's been hearing voices since he was a child. His parents also heard the voices of the dead. He did not commit the crimes of which he was accused and doesn't understand why he is in prison. Inmate Cabrera was apparently with some friends when they killed someone, and was convicted and sentenced to death for not trying to stop them.

I wonder how well any of the inmates' court-appointed attorneys represented them. I had worked with court-appointed pro bono attorneys before, who never met their clients until the day of the court hearing, and had already arranged a plea bargain before even hearing their stories. They can't really afford to spend much time with clients who can't pay them. The inmates say their lawyers often lie to them to get them to sign their plea bargains. They call these pro bono lawyers "public pretenders."

There are two more mattress fires the next day, and we're locked down on our wing again. Ms. Portland, who inhabits the office across from me, tells me this happens all the time – it's nothing to worry about. Inmates like to set their mattresses on fire. Nevertheless, the buzz with security is that these fires were coordinated efforts – the inmates are organizing for "something big."

There's a flood in Dr. Fielding's office downstairs. Inmate Cabrera is again accused of stuffing his blanket down the toilet in his infirmary cell, directly above her office. The inmate denies stuffing the blanket again.

Inmate Cabrera gets his medication once the head nurse returns as Dr. Steinberg predicted. However, he shows little improvement. He is still terrified of security, and believes they are now plotting to kill him in the gym. He knows this because he now hears the voice of another deceased friend, who has told him that security is still out to get him. He said that this friend, Juan, is much more reliable than Joey, the other deceased friend who visited with him before, and that he believes Juan totally. The inmate wants the doctor to know that he once practiced Santeria, and this is when he started hearing Joey. He was upset that he paid $20 to the Santero at the botanical store and ended up with Joey. Inmate Cabrera doesn't want to go to the CSU – he says he wants to go back to his "house." At this prison, the inmate's cell is called his "house." You hear workers asking inmates their house number rather than their cell number – one of the local euphemisms.

Dr. Steinberg noted that we have an ethical dilemma since someone with a chronic mental illness shouldn't have been sentenced to death. He asks the inmate his attorney's name. He is able to give the name and says that he has an appeal pending. Before inmate Cabrera leaves, Dr. Steinberg tells him that he is a very powerful Santero and will put a hex on anyone who tries to hurt him. The inmate smiles and seems to be comforted by this. Dr. Steinberg's quiet genius pops out unexpectedly. I see it a lot over the next few months. If he overmedicated people in his past life outside of prison, I can't believe it was motivated by profit.

34

Unlike most of the prison psychiatrists I've met, Dr. Steinberg really seems to care about his patients.

I speak with Dr. Fielding about inmate Cabrera and she warns me not to try to contact his lawyer as this would violate confidentiality. I wonder whose confidentiality she's talking about – the inmate's or the "System's?" I guess I already know the answer to that. The inmate surely would sign a release for me to talk to his attorney about something that would help his case – unfortunately the system won't. At my last prison, I was prohibited from talking or writing anyone outside the prison. Control is a big issue in prison – especially control of prison staff. There's a lot to hide here. I tell the inmate to make sure his lawyer gets his prison mental health records. I hope his attorney is compensated fairly for defending him on appeal.

September 2007

Our wing sergeant is rotated to a new assignment and we get a new sergeant who is actually rather pleasant. He has had marriage counseling and has some respect for mental health. He also seems to be into New Age spirituality – a rarity around here. We're in the South and most people around here are Southern Baptist or some variant thereof. He believes in treating inmates with respect. I wonder how he made it to sergeant in this crazy system. The sergeant invites us to share his coffee. Ms. Willert brings in flavored creamers and we build a relationship with our new security based around our shared coffee habit. I'm actually a tea drinker, but if coffee is disguised by the flavored creamers, I can like coffee too. I bring in a variety of flavored coffee too. The sergeant insists that his assistant always make the coffee. I notice he always gets the water from the hall closet. The new sergeant tells me that the faucet in the closet has a "super-filter" and that it is not safe to drink water from anywhere else. I suddenly get a sinking feeling in the pit of my stomach. Our previous sergeant said it was safe and I've been drinking out of the bathroom sink.

The psych. specs housed in the Old Laundry Room ask for a meeting about low morale and Dr. Fielding assembles all the psychologists and any psych specs who wish to attend in the conference room. Surprisingly, mostly only the psych specs from the Old Laundry Room show up. The Old Laundry Room workers were frightened that their prime office space might be taken from them. They heard the psychologists at the birthday party plotting to get it for ourselves.

Dr. Fielding establishes early on in the meeting that the psychologists need to stay on the wings with their staff, shooting down our hopes of increased safety and support. She asks for feedback on reasons for the low morale. Other than the obvious environmental factors and dangers inherent in our job duties, which no one bothers to mention, the psych. specialists extend their attack on the psychologists to more general issues, complaining that they don't feel the psychologists are pulling their weight. Some of the senior psychologists don't ever go out on the wings to see the inmates or help with the heavy load of paperwork. Psychologists in the prison system, I know from the reception center, have a reputation for being lazy or conducting their private businesses from their state jobs. I know that they have deadlines to keep up with here and can't really let things go. But I have heard that Dr. Davis refuses to go onto the wings with the inmates, and is in constant conflict with Dr. Fielding over that.

I bring up the smoking issue in the context of a health issue for inmates stuck on wings with no air conditioning or other ventilation. Dr. Fielding gives the standard reply that we must report any smoking on the wings to the warden. What did I expect? I also suggest that having the officers tell us on a daily basis that they don't want us here affects morale and creates a hostile work environment. They tell us gruesome stories about inmates to frighten us. I tell her that I had an officer, while laughing hysterically, tell me about an inmate who clamped his jaw around a psych specialist's breast and refused to let go. The officers tell us that something really bad is going to happen because security is more lax under this warden and they're losing control of the inmates. They sometimes leave the inside locks to the wings unlocked, leave mental health workers alone with inmates, fall asleep on the job, and don't monitor the "runaround" orderlies as they should. I'm not sure how much of the prediction that something bad is going to happen might actually be a threat.

Some of the psych. specialists suggest that security is just testing me because I'm new at State Prison. Another specialist says he's been there two years and they're still doing the same to him. I wonder if they want us gone badly enough to allow something to happen to get us to leave. Another specialist (who is rumored to have had a number of affairs with a variety of officers) says that the officers are very worried that something is going to happen because of the three fires. They feel the fires were a well-coordinated effort between three different wings. I'm thinking I know the first of the fire-setters. He does not speak English, and was too psychotic and afraid of everyone to be a part of such a thing. It's possible that the other two may have been in cahoots or they may have just been copy cats. Could these last two fires have been coordinated by security to scare us off? My level of distrust increases daily. Later in the week, two officers try to tell me there were actually ten fires –not three. Anything to increase the level of fear among the mental health professionals!

Dr. Fielding concludes the meeting by giving us her own method of maintaining morale. Every morning before going to work, she checks her retirement account. She has accrued $40,000 in the past two years.

Just as I'm mastering the routine paperwork, Dr. Fielding asks all of the case managers to refer any inmates who speak only Spanish to me since I'm the only mental health professional at this prison who speaks Spanish fluently. I wonder what they were doing prior to my arrival. I soon find out as I start seeing my Hispanic inmates. Inmate Cabrera wasn't the only psychotic Hispanic inmate at this prison. Just about everybody I saw was psychotic. Not knowing English, the isolation already imposed by their solitary cells was perhaps too much to retain their sanity – if they weren't already insane when they arrived.

So on top of all the other paperwork I had backing up, I had to meet with these inmates' psychiatrists and fill out the additional paperwork necessary to get them admitted to the hospital at an adjacent prison. Dr. Fielding soon adds one more task to my impossible list. She tells me that I need to work with Dr. Harmon on all the crisis cases involving Spanish-speaking inmates, so I need to start training with him.

Ms. Willert comes in upset that Dr. Pierkosky, has refused to medicate one of her inmates. The inmate is constantly getting into fights and has been unable to get out of confinement due to his temper. His mother keeps writing Ms. Willert, pleading with her to help him. She asks me to talk with Dr. Pierkosky.

I know Dr. Pierkosky by reputation already and meeting him only confirms my staff's report. He's the Polish-trained psychiatrist who seems to take great pleasure in berating the case managers at staffings. He begins by asking me where I was trained and lecturing me on how American mental health training is inadequate. Only European mental health professionals are competent. Obviously, I don't understand that this inmate is just antisocial. His anger is just a part of that. You don't medicate a personality disorder. I suggest that the inmate has concurrent issues that keep getting him in trouble, and that these can be helped with medication. Dr. Pierkosky takes great offense that I question his diagnosis and says he has work to do. So much for that! Maybe Ms. Willert's inmate can request a transfer to another psychiatrist.

I got a call from the Investigator General's office saying that a former employee at the reception center, Sheila Brown, had accused me of racial discrimination. She had accused one of my former psychological specialists of gender discrimination as well. This was a person Dr. Cramer had asked me to write up because she had had problems at the other two prisons where she had worked and had subsequently created problems working with my staff. She had phoned me after she was fired and told me that Dr. Cramer had said she was being terminated primarily because of what I had written about her. Why would he say such a thing? I wasn't even her primary supervisor and I certainly wasn't responsible for firing her. She was only assigned to me two days a week to help out with the heavy workload. I was set up! Even though she had no complaints about me when she was working at the reception center, she became upset by Dr. Cramer's statement that I was to blame for her termination, and filed a complaint against me. She called to ask me for a job reference, which I refused. I told her she needed to go through personnel for a reference. She probably wasn't too happy about that either.

I called Dr. Cramer and asked him what could happen as a result of this complaint and he said that I could probably be fired if it were validated. What is he saying? He knows it's not valid! I had gotten my staff to write statements about Ms. Brown's behavior before I left since she had accused more than one of my staff of some sort of discrimination, but I left the statements at the reception center for their protection. She did not at that time seem to have any complaint about me. When she had found out her primary supervisor wanted to fire her, she started accusing assorted staff of discrimination. I did not think at that time that I would need those written statements for my own protection. I called and asked that they be faxed to me.

I had a meeting with some people from the investigator general's office, and because I had an email from Dr. Cramer requesting that I write up the problems Ms. Brown had presented, showing that I had not initiated her termination, things were looking good for me. Not so much for my psych specialist though. I was told I'd get the outcome of the investigation within a month, but when I called over three months later before I left the job, I still was not given a judgment. I never did hear from them.

However, almost a year after I left the job, I heard from an attorney for the State and did have to be deposed on my psych specialist's case. I'm assuming the accusations against me were deemed unfounded since I wasn't being sued. The attorney for the State came to my office to meet with me prior to the deposition. We spent two hours talking – mostly about my experiences being harassed while working in the prison system. I was glad for the opportunity to vent and hoped what I said would somehow get back to the powers that be. I had thought of suing the State myself, but was ambivalent about that as I had seen many clients put their lives on hold for years because of lawsuits. I preferred to work. Also, my father, who was by then in his eighties, was terrified that they would burn down my house or hurt me in some way. I did eventually write several law firms about my difficulties, but no one wanted to represent me. I decided then to write a book about my experiences instead.

I had to give a deposition shortly thereafter at a neighboring prison. In the end, my psych. specialist's case settled and he kept his job.

Meanwhile, the building on my house had started. I was building a SIP home – the only one apparently in this county. I chose a SIP home due to their strength and good insulation. They're made of concrete board filled with four inches of foam and are said to resist up to 200 mph winds. After being hit by two hurricanes in my old home I was determined to build something strong this time. I had gotten free custom design services from the company that built the kit in return for the promise of writing an article about the house in the local newspaper. I took the article I wrote to the local weekly newspaper and the editor seemed excited, saying she would do a series of three articles at different stages of building the house.

I stopped at the local convenience store the next week to get the paper. The article on my house had not been published. I phoned the editor to see what had happened and she said that she hadn't been able to run this by Johnny. She promised to get with Johnny that evening and would be out the next day.

When I got home the next evening, the construction crew said the editor did not show up again. When I called her, she said that Johnny didn't want the article published. When I asked why, she said Johnny just wanted what was "best for the community." I asked her who Johnny was, thinking he must be the owner of the paper, and that I could perhaps talk with him about this. She replied that Johnny is the sheriff. So the sheriff in this county censors the newspaper - the craziness of the prison system extends into the community! Laws that apply elsewhere do not apply here!

I got a quote for $17,000 from a local contractor – just for framing the inside walls. Then I got a quote from a guy down the street for $3,000 for doing the same thing. Interestingly enough, when I tried to hire the guy down the street, he would not return my phone calls. Did someone get to him? Before I left the reception center, Dr. Cramer (who apparently had *some* redeeming qualities) urged me to sell my land and build elsewhere. He said that no one in this county, where over 90% of the people work for prisons, would help me. Apparently, they don't like mental health workers outside of prison either.

However, I had already fallen in love with the land and the house kit company was impatiently awaiting the opportunity to ship my house and threatening to charge me for storing my kit. I was going ahead with construction.

Over the next few months, I see that I should have followed Dr. Cramer's advice. The contractor I hired to pour the cement foundation got the location of the steel beams used to anchor the house somewhat off center. My engineer father insisted it wasn't a problem as the concrete under the beams was wide and went down two feet so basically it was all one piece – so no worries. I worried anyway, but it has held up fine in hurricanes and tornadoes so I guess he was right.

Two windows were in the wrong location so that they extended between two rooms, mostly where a wall dividing the rooms would be. This did have to be remedied, but the kit company, which cut them wrong, replaced them.

The tile guy bought 22 boxes of tile I didn't need, leaving them out in the rain so they couldn't be returned. Because he picked them up on a Saturday and didn't sign for them, I was not asked to pay for them. However, twenty-one pieces of expensive Italian trim disappeared while he was working on the house, and I had paid for those. The tile guy said he was helping a friend with a bathroom and was also remodeling his own bathroom so I guess that explains where that went. The tile store apparently blacklisted him, and he had to go to work subcontracting for one of the big hardware stores.

While I miraculously survived those blunders without great expense, others were costly. The air conditioning guy installed the air conditioner before the walls were put in so it had to be removed to finish the walls (I found out later that he had bought an air conditioner much too large for the well-insulated house and I had to exchange it as I was told it would have to work so seldom in my very insulated house that I would not have enough air circulation and would likely get mold).

The painter told me he needed a paint sprayer. I bought one and at the end of the day he told me it did not work properly and that I should take it back. This happened 3 days in a row, and at the end of these returns, the store cut my credit in half.

The workers stole everything but the kitchen sink (and that was only because I caught one of them trying to walk out with it). The painter did not caulk or prime the wood trim outside of the house and the paint soon peeled off.

I won't bore you with the many other problems these contractors gave me. However, it's important to note that after my painter brought a friend to build a porch railing, charged a bunch of tools that I did not authorize to my charge card, and disappeared without completing the job, I called the Sheriff's Office to make a report. A deputy came out and took my report. I also advised him of other things that had been stolen from the job and that pictures I had taken of the mess made by the air conditioning guys had been deleted from my camera. He told me to call the painter and let him know they needed to get back and finish the job or they would be arrested. I did so, but only got the painter's voice mail and left him messages.

I called the Sheriff's Office several times after this to let the deputy know the painter had not responded, but was never able to get in touch with the deputy and he never returned my calls. When I dropped by the Sheriff's Office and picked up a copy of the deputy's report (which labeled my report "inconclusive"), I was told that I would have to talk only to the deputy that took the report. No one else could do anything. Why exactly was that? This officer apparently only worked for the sheriff's office on the weekends. His other job was working as a prison inspector. I called his prison day job office and left a message, but as usual, got no response - ever.

I wrote a lengthy report of the many problems I had with my house construction and the sheriff's failure to respond as well as his censure of my newspaper article, and took this to the State's Attorney's office, but was told it wasn't their job to monitor the local sheriff's office. When asked whose job it was to monitor the sheriff's office, I was told I would need to contact the State law enforcement office. The State's Attorney's office said they could only make a courtesy call to the sheriff's office. I soon got a call from a deputy saying he would get my money back for me.

Unfortunately, I never did get my money back, and as usual, that deputy did not return my follow-up calls - ever.

I went to the State capital to report the problems to State law enforcement, but they told me that it wasn't their job to monitor the local Sheriff either. They told me there was an internal monitoring group inside the local Sheriff's office and I needed to notify them. In other words, the Sheriff's Department monitors itself. How convenient for them! I'm living alone in prison country and I'm wondering whether law enforcement here would even respond if I had an emergency. My father took me to a gun show and I bought a pistol. I've never been fond of guns, but I suspect I'm going to have to provide my own protection here.

My car broke down one weekend, and my tow truck driver, a man from Pakistan, told me that when he came to this country twenty years ago, he felt he was living in a democracy. Now, he sees the local sheriff's deputies following home drunk drivers who are native to this area, but arresting outsiders. He said that he once filed a complaint against his sheriff's department and found out soon enough not to do that again. He was given two speeding tickets (when he was not speeding). He thought he would be let off after explaining to the judge that the tickets were given in retaliation for his complaint against the Sheriff's office. After all they could have no radar readings to prove he was speeding, because he wasn't speeding. However, when he got to court, he was labeled a habitual offender, and the insurance rates on his tow trucks skyrocketed. I decided it might not be all that wise to file a complaint at the Sheriff's office when obviously no one else in the state was going to help me. Again, my elderly father urged me to let it go.

Did I mention that during this time, my apartment rent went up and on top of that, I was told that I would need to pay $200 per month per dog (but later found out my neighbors were told the fee was actually $20 per month)? Does the long arm of the prison system extend to my apartment? My clerk had told me she had friends who worked there – so maybe so.

I had acquired a stray dog that looked like a red wolf (and liked to run away at any opportunity) while visiting my father, and since my daughter had moved north and had no yard for her

Dalmatian, I had acquired him as well. Since I had land, I saw no reason to continue paying rent, built a fence around an acre of the property, and bought a used camper to live in. A burly neighbor, who worked at the prison where I first worked, saw me struggling to back the camper by the power pole, and heard the camper fall off the hitch with a loud thud. Apparently I hadn't secured it properly. He came over to help me move it and helped me hook the camper up to power. He was a sergeant at the prison, but hated his prison job – a good sign. This was just the beginning of many times this family helped me out before their daughter went AWOL and rejected them. Unfortunately, to get her back in their lives, they joined the neighbors in my harassment.

Camper living, I found, was not as much fun in the long run as it is for a weekend experience in the woods. My little camper was not very insulated and rocked in the high winter winds. Although I had left the land of frequent hurricanes, I found myself in the path of frequent tornadoes in the north of the state. During the first rain, I found that the camper also had several leaks, which were not easily sealed. My dog did not like being inside and confined herself to a small space in front of the door, but my daughter's large Dalmatian owned the place. He slept in my bed and growled at me when I tried to push him off my side. He beat me to the couch whenever I started toward it. I suppose I should be happy he allowed me in the camper at all, because he bared his teeth at anyone else who tried to get in the door. His white hair shed everywhere and he bled all over the rug when he cut his foot. My once cute camper soon was reduced to shambles. It got so cold in the winter that once the very insulated walls of the house were up, the dogs and I moved into the house at night. Getting up in the morning to run across the yard to the camper bathroom assured that I'd wake up faster than I might have liked, but at least I could sleep in the relative warmth of the house.

In spite of the difficulties of camping, I had fallen in love with the beautiful country around me. I didn't clear the back wooded acre of my lot, which went down to a little creek, and could frequently see deer and even the occasional fox running through there. The sunsets are beautiful here, especially after a rain. There are no tepid pinks or corals then, but bright, fiery,

44

orange skies that surround my home. If I did not know east from west, I couldn't have known it from the sky at sunset. A neighbor said that we have strange atmospheric conditions with unusual clouds here that give that surround sunset effect. While walking the neighborhood during one of these bright, fiery sunsets in the midst of my construction ordeal, I jokingly suggested to this neighbor that maybe this is "Hell, Florida."

We had a lot of tics in my wooded lot initially. I took my dog to a vet in a neighboring town to get her stitches removed after being spayed, and the assistant who saw me said my dog had some tics and that she would remove them. This seemed odd since I had just given the dog a bath and hadn't found any tics. Instead of using the usual tic removing instrument, she used a scalpel. When I got home and examined my dog, I could see that she actually had cut a gash under my dog's arm with the scalpel, and a large tic had crawled most of the way into the wound. She hadn't removed a tic; she inserted one into the cut she had made. This had to have been intentional! How do these people communicate? Am I on some sort of list? Do I dare take my animals to another vet here? Incidentally, I read online that bugs don't like garlic so I sprayed my trees with garlic juice and haven't seen a tic since. Why aren't we doing this in our parks?

October 2007

Meanwhile, back at the State prison, we have a new psychologist, Dr. Virginia Tremaine. She's very nice – seems unusually normal for this context. She's a tall, attractive young woman with an engaging smile, who is already gathering the interest of many security officers, especially our wing sergeant. She took my trainer, Dr. Sabine's contract position (but not her frequently absent staff, who stayed with me), so Dr. Sabine finally got to transfer to another prison in South Florida. I'd been so busy trying to take care of crises and Dr. Sabine was so busy job hunting that I never got much training in all the supervisory paperwork (not to mention that I was months without a working computer and never was given all the programs required to do my job).

Dr. Tremaine kindly drops by to offer help with paperwork. She only has three psych. specs to supervise and has time to learn the details from Dr. Fielding herself. I have double the number of psych specs (with double the paperwork), a bigger caseload, have to translate for the psychiatrists, and take care of any crises involving any Spanish-speaking inmates. Dr. Tremaine doesn't understand the imbalance in our workloads either. Maybe Dr. Fielding is trying to keep Dr. Tremaine from leaving by not overloading her from the start. She already knows I'm going to leave at the earliest opportunity.

I decide to talk to Dr. Fielding about reducing my caseload with all the additional duties I have by virtue of being bilingual. Dr. Fielding's response is noncommittal – everyone here is overloaded.

An officer in G wing complained that I was pulling out Inmate Cabrera on a weekly basis. Death row inmates require a two officer escort when they leave their cell and this leaves them short of staff. I pointed out to them that this inmate was in confinement, surrounded by people he could not communicate with since he only spoke Spanish, and was unstable enough to try to kill himself a few weeks before. The officer's comment was that he deserves to die – that everyone on their wing deserves to die. I remarked that often people who are mentally ill end up on their wing when they should really be in state hospitals where they can be medicated rather than being gassed when they act out. The officer argued that it doesn't matter that they are mentally ill – they still deserve to die for their acts. Later that day in the hallway, another officer from that wing, who had observed our conversation, stopped me and said that he did not agree with the officer who thought the mentally ill inmate deserved to die. He had worked at a state hospital and recognized that the mentally ill are not responsible for their actions when they are psychotic. It's a relief to know that not all of security is so jaded.

Inmate Cabrera asked for some books that might help him learn English. He's feeling very isolated with no Spanish speaking inmates housed near him. I check with the Education Department, but they have no books to teach English. I end up with some religious books in Spanish from the Chaplain. At least he'll have something to do in his cell. Ms. Portland tells me that death row inmates are entitled to a television and a fan. She says I need to get him a requisition form. I wonder why he hasn't been offered the television and fan before.

Ms. Portland had to go home because she sat on a batch of feces and semen on the group room bench. She said that some inmates will have sex anywhere they can. They tend to have poor judgment, however, as to whom to approach. One inmate almost got his penis bit off when he put it through the grate between the showers. The same thing happened when an inmate stuck his through the fencing in the recreation yard.

The next day, Ms. Portland asked me to accompany her to see an inmate she was concerned about. The inmate expressed a well-developed delusional system, in which he was called by God to communicate his version of Revelation to the world. He said that State Prison played a large part in the fulfillment of prophesy. He believed that when the saints come, there will be a battle against the "Black Beasts." He said he hated all Black people as the Bible told him to. There's so much to misinterpret in the Bible – such fertile grounds for psychosis! The inmate spent his days thinking of ways of killing the Black inmates around him. Ms. Portland said that the inmate in the cell beside him was from Haiti and practiced Voodoo, feeding her inmate's delusions. I asked the inmate if he would consider taking any medication. He said that he didn't like the way it made him feel. I suggested that he pray about it as everything has a purpose and we were with him for a reason. God may intend for him to take the meds. He's not convinced, but agreed to meditate on it. This inmate will be getting out in a few years. Even if he cannot behave himself well enough to get out of CM status by then, and cannot be trusted in a general prison population, he will be released to the public. He will go from the steel cell with the flap to freedom when his sentence is up. Ms. Portland and I go looking for his psychiatrist.

In the afternoon, Ms. Portland was doing rounds on our wing and saw a Hispanic inmate acting strangely. I went cell-front with her and the inmate raised up a cup to the window of his door and then drank from it. The corrections officer accompanying us yelled at him to put down the cup. He tells us the inmate has urine in the cup. I step back, wondering if he'll try to throw it at us. He doesn't. I tell the officer we need to have the inmate out to talk. Since the inmate speaks little English, I interview him. The officer warns me that he doesn't bathe and stinks. The inmate speaks very quickly. His answers to questions are so bizarre and unrelated to anything I ask that I have difficulty getting any information from him. Finally, he tells me that he drank his own urine so he will "be remembered." I wonder if he may be thinking of suicide, but he denies any suicidal thoughts. He speaks of his religion, Naningo, which he says is from Africa. He indicated that he had once eaten a man's heart after the man was killed in a religious ceremony. I asked him the significance of eating the heart, but he did not know. His clothes were dirty and he stank. I asked him if he bathed, and he said he did not like to shower because the water is cold. He claimed that he did wash off regularly. I've already been told some inmates won't go to the showers because they are so "nasty" with semen and feces everywhere. I take a referral to the psychiatrist's office. The nurse says he'll be seen in the AM.

I go back to my office and my stack of paperwork – now weeks old. I early on decided the many emergencies here have to come first. There's just not time to do all the paperwork required by the lawyers.

Fielding arranged a meeting with the warden to discuss the toilet paper issue among others. Toilet paper has become a scarce commodity. We've been told we will no longer be supplied garbage bags either. The State is short of funds. We're bringing in our own supplies. We bring in paper towels and liquid soap as well. Ms. Willert also brings in some baby wipes, but these tend to disappear over the weekends as these are highly prized among the inmates. The warden said we'd be allotted two rolls of toilet paper at a time. Soap was in short supply, but he was expecting to get some soon. We're allowed to ask questions of the warden, and I suggest we'd all feel safer and waste much less time if we did not have to depend on the key persons to get in and out of the wings. I ask if having keypads with hand print identifiers at each door like we use to check into the prison would be a breach of security. The warden said that there would be no problem with that, but that the cost was prohibitive - $2,000 per door. That did not seem like much considering that we can waste hours waiting on key people to appear, and officers have to be paid to run back and forth between doors on a daily basis. But then, of course, security would not have the control over mental health that they currently have.

Dr. Fielding asked that I have Mr. Kravatz, who is from Jamaica, check out the Haitian inmate lodged next to the psychotic hater of all Black people to see if he's also psychotic. Apparently, the inmate has been telling security that he practices Voodoo and that he's very powerful. It happens that Mr. Kravatz's aunt also practiced Voodoo and had taught him something about it. He said there really is a powder that turns people into zombies. The powder slows their pulse so much it can't be detected. The person is assumed dead and is buried. A few days later, they are dug up in zombie state and used as slaves. An officer asks if there's anything a person can wear to protect himself from voodoo. Mr. Kravatz responds that there is nothing one can wear – like a cross – for protection. You just have to be virtuous – act right and you'll be protected. Mr. Kravatz points out that people apprentice in voodoo and have to learn from the oral tradition as nothing is ever written down. After assessing the inmate, he decides that he is not psychotic. He has been actually trained in Voodoo. This leaves security nervous.

I have another inmate that needs hospitalization. He's been refusing meds since he was last released from the hospital about a year ago. He told me that he sees and hears people from the president's office, who insert thoughts in his brain. He also has ulcers, which he attributes to psychological experiments that he believes have been conducted on him. He doesn't want to go back to the hospital. He offers to take meds as long as they won't keep him awake. Dr. Fielding wants me to refer him to the hospital anyway so I fill out the paperwork. Hopefully, his fears will be medicated away before his transfer to the hospital comes through.

Ms. Portland tells me that a number of inmates have seen ghosts in their cells. Security has also seen the ghosts and has had to move inmates because the ghosts of the deceased inmates didn't want to share their cells. I remember reading a John Edwards' book that said we shouldn't be executing inmates for that precise reason. They tend to hang around and be a nuisance. We should instead be focusing on rehabilitating them.

Dr. Cramer, the regional consultant, calls asking me to put in for a transfer to State Prison. I am only there on "temporary assignment." I tell him I might transfer if I can get a raise. He says he doubts it, but he'll check into it for me. Maybe I could tolerate this place a few more years and earn some retirement if he made it worthwhile. The Hispanic inmates obviously need someone they can communicate with.

I'm in an interview room with a CM-I inmate, when he points out that the officer "sitting on him" has fallen asleep outside the door. The inmate lets me know that he could do anything he wanted to me before the officer would even wake up. Ms. Portland later tells me the same officer has fallen asleep while she was meeting with inmates as well. He is a young man, who likes to brag about his all night sexual exploits, and sleeps through most of his day job. I'm still reeling from my problems with security at the reception center. I don't need any problems with security here. I don't file a complaint. I just wake up the officer.

I also knew that filing an incident report didn't mean anything would be done. My clerk at the reception center used my computer code to change an inmate's classification, which affected where he would be placed and whether he would get psychiatric care. The computer tech called to tell me about this and I filed an incident report (which is supposed to go to the state office in Tallahassee). My staff said that people are typically fired for this type of fraud. When I called to see what happened with this incident report, I was told that they had had a "good talk" with my clerk and she said she wouldn't do it again. They rewrote my incident report (and did not show it to me) so she wouldn't get fired.

I wait to get in G wing with the education specialist, a young woman who tells me she is "gunned" every day. She said she doesn't understand why she gets all the attention. She's overweight and doesn't think she's very attractive. She has to go cell-front to give out and collect paperwork. She said she just keeps her eyes forward and ignores it. She's a single parent and can't afford to take the pay cut that teaching at a public school would mean. The officers don't want to deal with the paperwork of constantly writing up these guys.

Later that morning, while I'm waiting for an officer to get an inmate I need to interview, I'm left by myself on the quarterdeck. I notice the runaround peering over the stair railing at me from the stairs between the first and second floors. I see his hand bobbing up and down – another gunner! I get up and run to the stairs. He runs up faster than me. I yell up that he better run away. Like my prior gunner, this inmate is running toward security for protection. I'm angry now. I tell the officer what happened when he comes back. This officer is an older man, who seems sympathetic. He says he'll take care of him. Apparently taking care of him meant protecting him from me, because he was still on the wing the next time I went to that wing. The inmate did make a point of avoiding me after that though. Both of the "runaround" inmates who flashed me were little, effeminate guys that I thought certainly must be gay. I don't think they had any interest in flashing a woman. Security must have put them up to it.

November, 2007

My death row inmate never made it to the Crisis Stabilization Unit at our neighboring prison. I continue meeting with him every week. Today they don't take us to the usual room in the hallway where the two guards stand outside the door. They take us instead to a room downstairs in their own wing. Inmate Cabrera asks that I teach him some English. He wants to know how to ask for a cigarette and how to tell someone that he owes him cigarettes. The inmate also wants me to translate a letter from his lawyer relating to his appeal. I translate the letter for him and notice as I look out the window of the room that the guards have disappeared. The inmate notices too and tells me that he will not treat me with disrespect (gun me) as the other inmates left alone with women mental health workers do. He respects me "like a mother." I trust the inmate, crazy as he is, more than the guards. I see now why they brought us to this isolated room with no witnesses. I wonder how they reward the inmates for gunning the women here - a few cigarettes? When the guards finally showed up, I heard the inmate say as they walked up the stairs, "You owe me a cigarette." I guess they don't have cameras in that room.

Dr. Fielding announced that our district manager is coming to audit charts. We need to get caught up. My crew is 50 documents behind even though two months ago, they had all caught up for the last audit. Dr. Fielding wants to know why my guys are so far behind. Some of them like to talk, I know. The stress here makes people want to seek support, but there's no time. But that's not what caused this back up. I remind Dr. Fielding that the 50 documents due appeared when she had the computer program corrected. Interestingly enough, the other psychologists only had two or three that showed up. Was this computer glitch really an accident? My staff started staying late again to catch up. I stay until 8 pm trying to help them with their documents. I get more than thirty of the documents done myself that week. My staff gets the rest done. We are caught up!

The day before everything's due, Dr. Fielding emails me that she needs my chart reviews and supervision sheets as these will also be reviewed by the district mgr. It's finally catching up with me – that elusive paperwork. I write her back that I was told the supervision paperwork was last priority and that I had focused on helping staff catch up with their documents as required by the lawyers. She said I'd still have to do them. No sympathy there. There's no time left. They won't get done. She doesn't seem upset. They're probably not part of the review.

I've been crying on the way to work every day for two weeks. I can diagnose myself when something inside me starts welling up and I now meet criteria for Major Depressive Disorder. Did it begin when I told Dr. Cramer I might stay at this most horrible of prisons? Maybe it's a realization that I really am getting older and may never be able to retire. After all, I came to prison to work long enough to earn a retirement I could live on. But I can't stay at this prison much longer. They're going to keep leaving me alone with inmates, and the next one may not be as appropriate as my death row inmate. Death row inmates have nothing to lose; they've already been sentenced to death. New charges aren't going to get them any more punishment. I'm so discouraged. I should have stayed in South Florida where people are saner.

Dr. Fielding announces at staff meeting that if Dr. Finley asks them to do anything on a chart, then they need to do it because that is one of the charts that will be reviewed. I can't believe she's admitting that she created a false crisis here, telling staff they had to have all their charts done for this review when actually she knew all along which charts were needed. My staff are furious. I'm not too happy myself. Those supervision checklists she said she had to have were probably also a hoax. OK, all bets are off. I no longer feel obligated to stay late to get all this paperwork done. I'm exhausted at the end of a normal day.

I visit my death row inmate Cabrera, who seems to be worse today. Security tells me he's been on his knees praying most of the day. The inmate says the other inmates made a ruckus on Sunday night, and he knows it's because they want to kill him. I suggest the football game was likely involved in the ruckus. He didn't buy this and said that he had heard that the bounty on his head was raised to $54,000. I assured him no one here had that kind of money to put a bounty on his head and that if anyone told him about a bounty, they were lying to him. I suggest he might feel safer in the hospital. I call Dr. Fielding and tell her I think Inmate Cabrera needs to transfer out to the hospital since he seems to be deteriorating. She was in agreement and said to try to get Dr. Steinberg to sign off on this one. She said to tell him there's already one death row inmate at the hospital with an officer one-on-one with him so he could stand watch over both of them. When I talked with Dr. Steinberg, he said he was OK sending Inmate Cabrera to the hospital since there would be an officer available to watch him. He said his hesitance in sending him before was because he was afraid the inmate might hurt someone over there due to his paranoia.

I get an inmate complaint claiming that Mr. Kravatz made sexual advances towards him. He claims Mr. Kravatz told him he'd like him to come out of his cell and expose his genitals to him. This inmate had "gunned" a female case manager and I imagine Mr. Kravatz was expressing his anger at the inmate for his behavior, and looking for an opportunity to dissuade him from doing this again. I'm told to write an incident report and that Internal Investigations will handle it. Mr. Kravatz is on vacation so I can't tell him what's happening. Inmates tend to make false complaints whenever they want a change in case managers. This inmate is probably hoping to be assigned a woman again.

Dr. Cramer calls wanting to know why I haven't put in for a transfer to State Prison. The reception center can't hire anyone until I leave the position there and they don't want me back. I tell him that I was waiting to hear if I was getting a raise. He says there's no money – the State is bankrupt. There's no other place close by that I can go to. My heart sinks. At least I've identified the source of my depression. I reluctantly tell him I'll send in the transfer papers. Why did I do that? If I request a transfer, I'm stuck here for a year. The State will only allow one transfer a year. I tell myself I am not imprisoned here. There are other jobs out there. I just might have to travel farther. Dr. Tremaine drops by to check on me. She's worried about me – I can tell. I manage a smile through teary eyes.

I phone personnel asking that they put a hold on my transfer. I call Dr. Cramer and let him know that I didn't want to request the transfer because I didn't want to be stuck at State Prison for a whole year. He said I wouldn't need to be stuck there. He can move me at any time. I told him I knew that wouldn't happen. They can't get anyone to take my place. I told him he could transfer me to State
Prison if he wanted, but I wouldn't be putting in for the transfer. I didn't ask to be assigned here and I didn't want to stay here. He warned that the reception center would have to give a reason if they requested the transfer. I asked him what reason that might be and he said it would be something like "supervision" and that this would come from my supervisor there, the warden, and the hospital administrator. I said I'd like to see them do that. I had a huge pile of forms documenting supervision at that job. No one had told me there was a standard supervision form and I created my own. The standard form, which I was shown when I moved to the State Prison, would not have been appropriate for the intake unit anyway. We didn't have ongoing cases; we only saw the inmates once for intake. I told Dr. Cramer I was planning to leave as soon as I could find a job – hopefully in January when I'll be vested to retire. He suddenly switched gears and said that "we

always lose our best people." I'm thinking they'll probably wait to see if I leave in January.

I'm eager to start my job search. Nothing much shows up on the internet – just prison jobs for psychologists. I had worked almost nine years doing social security evaluations for the Department of Health prior to taking the prison job. I call my old scheduler at the Department of Health to see if there might be any work available in this area. She refers me to the professional relations person, who was excited that I speak Spanish and have experience. They just happen to need someone. I tell her I just have to wait until January when I can be vested for retirement. I call personnel and am told I'll qualify for about $200/month retirement on January 1. If I'd have stayed ten years with prison retirement, I would have qualified for many times that. So, I'll work forever...

December, 2007

Dr. Cramer emailed me asking if I'd commit to staying a year or two if he got me the 10% raise and the incentive pay. I told him I was waiting to hear about some contract work and planning to leave in January. As much as I hated being there, I didn't want to leave the Hispanic inmates without any care. I offered to stay on part-time to see the Spanish speaking inmates. He said he'd think about it.

At a staff meeting in the Old Laundry Room, Dr. Fielding tells us that the warden has sent out a warning that they'll be searching our vehicles. No weapons should be left in the backs of trucks; no drugs should be left in cars. A psych specialist jokes that he covers his with a blanket and never has any problem. The proximity of Xmas seems to have lightened everyone's mood. They say this place grows on you. In a weird way it does. People bond together against the ever dangerous environment and the ever impossible workload. I'll miss that when I go back in business on my own.

Our E-wing sergeant was trying to make lieutenant, which he had put off for years until his daughter was older as it would likely mean he'd have to move out of the area. He had asked me to write him a letter of recommendation, which I cautioned might actually hurt him more than it would help coming from me, but I wrote it anyway. He had an easy way with the inmates. He did not believe in harassing them and they responded well to him. Our wing was usually quiet. He didn't make lieutenant, probably because he emphasized that he got along well with mental health. We threw him a party anyways to tell him we appreciate his help. Relations with security are vital here and ours is good with our present security staff. There's something about sharing coffee together that helps too – maybe our mutual dependence gives us a common denominator. The Sergeant still insists that he wants his man to make the coffee. He won't drink it if anyone else makes it because he wants to make sure the water comes from the sink in the closet with the "super filter."

Our sergeant almost got thrown over the railing during a cell extraction (an inmate refused to leave his cell and had to be forcibly removed). The other officers came to my office window (I now have Dr. Sabine's office) to watch as they walked the inmate down the hallway to the clinic. The inmate looked pretty battered. I said it looked like they gave him a real beating. The officers laughed and said they never "beat up" inmates – they were just responding to the inmate's attack and it all occurred during the process of "restraining" the inmate.

Dr. Cramer calls wanting to know my plans. I tell him I'll let him know when I've signed a contract. He says he still doesn't know if he can get me adequate pay to stay on part-time to see the Hispanic inmates. I tell him to let me know. Shortly thereafter, Dr. Fielding tells me they'll be transferring out the Hispanic inmates who don't speak English. There's a maximum security prison down South where a number of employees speak Spanish. I'm relieved; I'll be totally out of here!

Christmas 2007

I'm invited out of town to have Christmas with friends. I make brandied sweet potatoes and a casserole my grandmother used to make. I'm greeted with a feast at the friends' house. There are beautiful, yeast rolls, which I have to try. However, immediately thereafter, I could feel myself bloat, and I continued to bloat and bloat. I wasn't able to eat for the next two days. I'd never had that sort of reaction before. Nobody else had a problem with the yeast rolls. Why is my body acting this way when we have all these wonderful leftovers to eat?

January 2008

Dr. Steinberg gives me a page from a book he's writing. I'm apparently not the only one documenting the craziness here. He says that psychiatrists who work at prisons all get SPD – Stupid Psychiatrist Disease. They stereotype and treat all prisoners as if they are malingering – faking illness to manipulate and secure some type of secondary gain. He says I'm unusual in that I haven't become jaded by prison.

Well, the accident waiting to happen did. When I got back from Xmas vacation, there was an email indicating that there was a meeting with the warden while I was out – to discuss the "incident." No one was on my hall yet so I phoned Dr. Fielding to ask her about it. She said that Ms. Baxter, a case manager, was assaulted. Dr. Fielding said that she didn't know the details of what had happened, but said that "these things very rarely happen at prisons." She said that Ms. Baxter was not hurt physically, but was shook up, and had not yet come back to work.

Ms. Willert and Ms. Portland came in together with the details. Ms. Willert was actually on H wing at the time of the "incident." H wing is a CM-3 wing and the inmates are not cuffed when we see them. The officer, who was supposed to be "sitting on the inmate" for Ms. Baxter, had wandered off. No officers were on the quarterdeck at the time. Ms. Willert called for the officers when she heard Ms. Baxter's screams. The inmate was trying to rape her. Two officers came and tried to restrain the inmate, but he broke loose and attacked Ms. Baxter again. He threw her against the wall and scratched her face. When the officers pulled him off her again, Ms. Willert grabbed Ms. Baxter and took her to the door to the hallway. Fortunately, the door was unlocked from the inside, which probably saved them all. Ms. Willert started banging the door until some officers in the hallway unlocked the door from the outside and helped take down the inmate.

There was a meeting with the warden to discuss the incident, but this simply served to infuriate all the mental health staff – except for Dr. Fielding, who steadfastly maintained the party line as usual. When mental health staff complained that they are frequently left alone with inmates, the warden faulted them for not reporting this problem sooner. Of course, we all know that our lives depend upon those officers we would be reporting. The warden told the mental health staff that they get extra pay for a reason and that in a prison they can expect some problems. There was no mention of security's responsibility for not following procedure. Not only did the officer leave Ms. Baxter alone with the inmate, they did not call for backup. The officer who left his post was not disciplined; he was at work the next day.

I was sick my last week of work. It had rained hard and some coffee colored liquid was on the floor of my office when I went in. Breathing it in burned my throat. All of the prisons in the area were built with flat roofs and apparently millions have been spent trying to fix them to no avail. I shudder to think what would happen if a hurricane or tornado hit this feeble prison and these psychotic inmates were set loose on the area. I moved to the empty office down the hall, but the next day I was too weak to go in to work and had developed a bad cough. When I came back a week later to empty my office (still weak and coughing), all the pictures I had on my bulletin board had faded. What was that coffee-colored stuff?

A little bit of mercy makes the world less cold and more just.
Pope Francis

Chapter II

Poisoned in Prison

That uncomfortable experience with yeast rolls the Christmas of 2007 was only the beginning of my digestive problems. I became increasingly sensitive to gluten and lactose over the next couple of years, and could expect to get sick any time I ate out. I eventually figured out I was sensitive to chlorine in city water as well. I was so drained I could barely stay awake at work and slept any hours I wasn't working. I tried to get an appointment with the local naturopath, but he was booked, so I went through my health plan to a conventional MD. His great insight was that I was getting older and could expect to be less tolerant of certain foods. Upset by this nonexplanation, I began doing some research of my own on the internet. I found a site where people were saying they had cured their digestive problems with food grade peroxide. I started treating myself with peroxide and soon could see that my problem was coming from parasites. Once I began the treatment (a few drops of peroxide in distilled water), I was able to eat again without getting sick. My neighbor told me that he had a friend who had gotten parasites from the water at the death row prison. So that's why they had the super filter. They knew the water was toxic! That first sergeant on the wing intentionally poisoned me, telling me the water was safe to drink. I decided I needed to get tested to document this.

January 2010

I called my local health department to see if they did parasite testing. They referred me to a larger health department in Gainesville so I phoned to request a parasite sample kit. I was told there would be a kit for me at the front desk if I wanted to pick it up the next day.

I went to the Health Department to pick up the sample kit. Without looking, the receptionist said, "There's nothing here for you-oo." When I asked her to look, she quickly turned her head to the side and back, saying sarcastically, "There's nothing here." Another woman pushing a cart came by and said she'd talk with the assistant director. She came back and said that they do not do testing without a doctor's orders. I told her I knew that was not true. I had lived out of the country and had been tested at health departments before when I was back in the States. Besides, I had already been told I could pick up the kit here.

I phoned the epidemiologist on her next working day, and she confirmed that they do testing without doctor's orders and said that I should come back and get the kit directly from her. A friend, Martha, was also having some digestive problems and wanted tested. I asked Irene if she would give my kit to Martha, who would be coming by to get a kit for herself. She agreed to do so.

I picked up the kit from Martha, who said that Irene told her my kit had been at the front desk all the time. When I opened up the kit to read the directions later that evening, I saw that the directions did not match the number of containers in the bag. I phoned Martha to see how many containers were in her package. Martha said there were four and that we were to use two of them on two separate days. I only had three containers.

I phoned epidemiologist, Irene, again, and she indicated that I should have had four containers. She told me she did not want to leave anything at the front desk for me again, and that I should come directly to her to pick up the container. I picked up the fourth container from Irene. She told me she did not know what had happened with that kit. She said it had been at the front desk all the time. The bag had been stapled shut. She asked me to deliver the sample directly to her hands.

I obtained a sample with long, spaghetti-like, easily visible worms in it, and took the sample directly to Irene. Surely, they could not miss these parasites. Irene said it typically takes 7-10 days to get the test results. I called her a week later and she said the sample had just been sent to the lab. I asked her why it had sat there a week before they sent it to the lab. She did not know.

Irene phoned the next day saying my test results were negative for both parasites and bacteria. She said she was able to get the results from the computer. I asked her how the results could come in so quickly and how they could be negative when the parasites in the sample were visible to the naked eye. She did not know. She suggested I see an infectious disease specialist and gave me some names. My friend, Martha, had not yet received her test results.

I called the infectious disease specialists Irene had referred me to. Two of them had retired; the other said I would need to be referred by my primary doctor. My primary would have to test me and find parasites. I phoned my HMO to get a new doctor, and made an appt.

The new doctor could not fathom why the health department would wait a week to send off the sample and did not believe the health department could have gotten the results in such a short time after finally sending it to the lab. She ordered retesting. I recognized a high-ranking officer from the prison following me in when I picked up the kit from the lab. I already knew this was probably futile, but took my new sample to a lab in Jacksonville, thinking maybe I could get accurate results if I went out of town.

My friend Martha called saying she had finally received her test results from the health department. She faxed them to me showing her negative results. Interestingly enough, her results had the name of a different county health department near the State capital – not the one where we both went. She told me she had been constipated and hadn't taken in her sample until a week after I did. In fact, she took her sample in the day mine was sent off. It was only later after she started behaving strangely that I wondered if it hadn't been her sample that was sent in my name.

After I left prison, I started up my own business, and during this time, I had allowed this friend, Martha, to use my office one evening a week. She said she was having financial problems and was giving up her business. She just had a few clients to finish up with. One day I found the key to my office in the kitchen of the office building. I had suspected someone else was using my office during the days I wasn't there. I'd come in and the fan was set on high (I always had it on low and Martha shut it off altogether) or I'd find that a new ink cartridge in my printer was totally used up. One day that I did not typically work in that office, I dropped by to pick up some papers and heard male voices in my office. By the time I got in, they had run out the back door.

Martha called the day I found the keys in the kitchen, and said she needed to come in early to see a client. This was not the evening that I had told her she could use the office. She said she had picked up some new clients and she was now using the office three evenings a week. I advised her that if she was again building her business and using the office three days a week that I would need her to pay a share of the rent. When she got to the office, she insisted that I leave the keys I had found there for the landlord to check it out. It later occurred to me that she could be renting out my office on days I was working out of town, leaving these keys in the kitchen for someone else to use. Maybe she came in early while I was there because she didn't have her keys. In any case, she refused to pay any rent and I advised her she would need to find herself a new office.

During the months she had used my office, I thought we had become close friends. I had confided to her problems I had been having with my daughter, and she confided in me problems she was having with her husband and at her part-time jobs. Often when she called me, she would quickly say she forgot to do something and ask me to call her back in five minutes. When I would call back, the answering machine would pick up before she picked up, and she would laugh and announce that I was being recorded. I would tell her I had nothing to hide. After a few times of this happening, I noticed the answering machine never turned off as they tend to do after a few minutes. She was recording the entire conversation. I stopped calling her back.

Martha refused to pay rent or move out of the office and I had to enlist the landlord's help to get her out. She called me saying she couldn't afford to pay rent, but in the next sentence she said she had to dip into savings to pay the mortgage that month. She had savings? She had told me she was broke and her husband wasn't making any money! Why had she recorded our conversations? Was she somehow connected to the prison? Or did I just have incredibly bad luck?

My new doctor called after a week saying that my test results were negative. Soon after, I was able to get in to see a naturopath. While he thought I had probably gotten rid of the parasites with the peroxide I had taken since I could eat again without getting sick, the parasites can still remain hidden - dormant in the body for years. He thought the residual poisons were probably causing the exhaustion I was still experiencing. I needed IV glutathione treatments to get rid of the poisons. Prior to this I would need a series of extensive (and expensive) testing to see what was out of whack in my body. I would also need to check the well water at my home to make sure it wasn't toxic. I'm wondering how I can get my well water mailed off to be tested without some security officer following me into Fed Ex. I suspect I failed at that since my well water results came back with nothing elevated even though I have so much iron in my water that I'm constantly battling those orange stains in my bathtub and toilets.

An interesting result of all that testing by my naturopath showed that I had no lithium. I didn't actually know that I needed any. As far as I knew lithium was a strong substance used to treat people with Bipolar Disorder. My naturopath told me there were studies in Texas showing that five major crimes increase in areas where there is no natural lithium in the soil and water. People get very anxious and impulsive without lithium. Maybe that's why we have the murder of the day on the local news! It was reported that amounts as low as 20 mcg per day (not the dangerously large doses of lithium prescribed by MD's) could make a huge difference.

Florida has no natural lithium in its soil and water. Anyone who lives here any amount of time will become low in lithium. Can this be why I see people with symptoms of Bipolar Disorder every day here in North Florida where families have lived for generations, but rarely saw them when I worked in South Florida, where people came from all over the country and most people I saw were not native to this State? What a simple solution. The health department could provide lithium supplements to people. Crime would go down. Oh, I forgot. The prison system's goal is self-perpetuation. Who really wants the crime rate to go down?

I eventually wrote the new governor to advise him of the parasites I had contracted in prison and the difficulties I experienced in dealing with the health department. I got an email back from someone with the State Department of Health, apologizing for the difficulties I encountered at the health department. She said no one remembered me after all this time; I should have written sooner. Sorry, I was too busy mustering up enough energy to make it to work with parasites eating me up. The rest of my life was spent sleeping. And I had already written the former Governor about problems with the prison system, and got no response. I'm excited to have gotten any kind of response this time - even that response.

The Department of Health referred me to someone at the Department of Environmental Regulation. He seemed upset that I had written the governor. I should have contacted him directly. I told him of my experience with the County Health Department. He said I couldn't possibly have contracted parasites from the prison water because they *hyper-chlorinate* the water in that prison. He said I would *just* have gotten *cancer* from the disinfection byproducts – not parasites. In any case, I would only have gotten cancer if I had been exposed to the water for fifteen years or more. There was nothing to worry about since I was only there a short time. They started hyper-chlorinating the water in the early 2000's. He said security initially complained they would have to bring in bottled water and wanted compensated for that expense, but of course they weren't. I advised him that they now have filters. He said he would check the water again. I suggested he make sure he got the water from a sink without a filter.

Sadly, it appears no one cares if the inmates are being poisoned. Death row inmates (many of them as I found were psychotic and didn't belong on death row) can stay there for 20 or 30 years before they're executed – plenty of time to get cancer from the water if they're not eaten up by the parasites first.

It was several months after my glutathione treatments that I started noticing those familiar symptoms again. The buggers didn't stay dormant for long. I read about a company that did DNA parasite testing in a health newsletter I subscribe to. I called my naturopath and he ordered the testing. I not only drove two hours away, but borrowed my father's car to take the sample to Fed Ex this time. Success at last! The results came back with three types of parasites. One was typically water-borne, one was contracted from direct contact with excrement or the soil (perhaps like Ms. Portland, I encountered some excrement on a poorly cleaned prison bench), and the last one was "unknown." Maybe that last one is the scariest. What is it and is there a way to get rid of it?

I emailed the person who had written me from the State Department of Health to let her know I had been successful in identifying the parasites. This time I got no response. I called the guy from Environmental Services and he laughed when I told him I had three types of parasites. He said he once had parasites and had a hard time making it to the bathroom. I told him it appeared that his hyper-chlorination wasn't killing all the bugs – at least some were getting through. He then declared sarcastically that I couldn't prove I got the parasites from prison; I could have gotten them anywhere. The fact that I started getting sick when I was at the prison with water so contaminated that it requires hyper-chlorination is only coincidental, I guess.

My naturopath started treatment with Oregano Oil, which I was unable to take at the prescribed level and still work with the severe diarrhea it brought on. I took it at a level I could tolerate for a month, but I still had symptoms. I attended a workshop with a variety of alternative health professionals, who all had their recommended cures. I tried them all, but was still exhausted and experiencing digestive problems, and went for frequency specific microcurrent treatments. The hyper-chlorination must have produced treatment-resistant bugs. I went back to my naturopath, who suggested a combination treatment and reordered testing. I did not feel I had gotten rid of all the buggers even after the combination treatment. I cancelled my next two appointments and postponed the testing until after Christmas while I continued treatment.

A few months later when I felt I had gotten rid of the buggers and was recovering energy, I retested, but was surprised to find out that I had two types of blood borne parasites (one still there from prison) as well as another intestinal parasite. One of the blood borne parasites, curiously enough, is contracted from snails that hang out in the waters of Africa, Brazil, and a few islands I've never been to. The only place I could have contracted them was Brazil and I was last there as a child. These shistosomes are supposed to be vicious buggers who end up shutting down the liver and killing you. Have they been dormant in my body all these years? Maybe the frequency treatments set lose some encapsulated bugs. Or maybe someone messed with my testing again! Those shistosomes would have had to have appeared in the first DNA testing if they had been there since childhood, wouldn't they?

My naturopath spoke to the lab and suggested they may have goofed, but they insisted DNA testing is infallible. I talked to one of the Juvenile Justice guys at my office and he said the FBI makes mistakes in their DNA testing all the time. Nothing's infallible. My naturopath ordered some blood testing at a local lab to confirm the parasites. The testing was inconclusive. He offered to send me to an infectious disease specialist. I researched the standard medical cures which are pretty toxic and only work about 70% of the time, and decide I'll just treat myself with some different natural cures just in case I still have some parasites. However, I'm not feeling bad anymore and I suspect it likely that someone again tampered with my test results.

Science without religion is lame;
religion without science is blind.

Albert Einstein

Our scientific power has outrun our spiritual power. We
have guided missiles and misguided men.

Rev. Martin Luther King, Jr.

Only two things are infinite, the universe and human
stupidity, and I'm not sure about the former.

Albert Einstein

Chapter III

Social Security

The first office I rented when I opened my business doing social security evaluations was in a small group of buildings conveniently located by a bus stop. Many of the people I saw for social security did not own cars and I needed to be near a bus stop. I also needed a handicap accessible bathroom, which I found was in short supply in offices in the City of Gainesville. I felt fortunate to have fairly quickly located this office. However, my first day working, I was met by another tenant, who announced that he did not like the looks of my clientele and that I would have to move out. He had a small business catering to wealthy clients and they would not like coming to his office if they saw my clients hanging around. I advised him that I had no intention of moving and that if he did not like my clientele, then *he* might like to move somewhere else. In any case I had a six month lease and could not believe that this bigot could influence the landlord to make me move. It turns out I was wrong about that. The landlord called saying he saw one of my clients smoking in the parking lot and that he could not have that. I would have to find another office which met the bus and bathroom requirements. This was not at all easy to do and I ended up in an older house shared by a number of therapists for two years until I found a more private office.

I had an unusual number of people who went through the long process of applying for social security, but did not show up for their appointments. My first year and a half in business, I accumulated five boxes of no show files – appointments I did not get paid for. These were only the no shows that *never* showed up. Many others were rescheduled, came to their second appointments, and were filed with the kept appointments. I figured I actually got paid for less than half the clients that had scheduled appointments.

In my nine years doing the same work in the southern part of the state, I had only accumulated a couple of boxes of no show files. What was going on here?

I also had a rash of clients who called repeatedly, interrupting my work asking for directions to my office. They would try to keep me on the phone while they drove to the office. If I told them I could not stay on the line and hung up, they would immediately call me back – over and over again. This seemed rather strange behavior for people who were depending on me to get approved for disability. This was happening several times a week - something that rarely happened when I was working in South Florida. I had to stop answering the phone at all during the day and left my voicemail to give directions.

I called to see if the local medical transport company could bring someone to my office, and was told that they could no longer do so. They said that because I was not actually providing treatment, but just evaluating people, they could not provide services to my office. I asked if there were other doctors that they couldn't take people to see and they said I was the only one. Come on! I know several doctors doing the same type of evaluations.

I also had a few people file ridiculous complaints against me, which fortunately my professional relations person with the state could see through. It was obvious that there were people who wanted to keep making things harder for me after I left prison.

In my social security practice, I often see inmates trying to get disability after they leave prison. The mental health centers have lost funding to see people without income or Medicaid. Without medication and unable to find work with their felony records, some have narrowed their lives and stay at home so they won't get in trouble again. They know if they violate probation they'll go back to prison for a year and a day. Others go back to illegal drugs in an attempt to self-medicate their psychiatric problems. I tell them about natural alternatives (citing research only; I'm not allowed to make recommendations) to the prescription drugs they can't afford, but they usually can't afford those either.

Kevin had spent a year and a day in prison on a violation of probation charge. He had only been sentenced to community service and three years' probation for his possession of marijuana charge. But then he violated probation by not paying his child support (he had lost his job when he was arrested) and ended up with a year and a day in prison. He hadn't been able to find work since his release and was having nightmares about being arrested and sent back to prison again for still not being able to pay his child support. He hid behind dark curtains at his house, jumping every time the dog barked, thinking the police were coming to take him back. His only hope was to qualify for disability as this would excuse him from paying the child support. He cried as he related his story. He couldn't tolerate going back to prison. He was only twenty seven years old and had never been in trouble other than the marijuana charge. Now it looked like he'd be one of those caught in the revolving door of the criminal justice system.

Johnny came in threatening suicide if he did not get approved for disability. He was tired of living in a tent in the woods. He had never been able to hold a job for more than six months. He'd been to prison seven times for a variety of violent charges and had never been diagnosed with the Bipolar Disorder that was behind his impulse control problems. He was determined not to go back to prison again. He only left his tent to go to a shelter to bathe in the early afternoons when no one was there. He could not be around people for long without getting into a fight. His voices told him people were talking about him and making fun of him. His mother dropped off food for him, but could not live with his temper. He had never been properly diagnosed or treated for his Bipolar Disorder, and I knew that without any documented history, he'd be unlikely to be approved even with my diagnosis. A couple months later confirmation came that he had not been approved. His mother called accusing me of killing him. Apparently he committed suicide when he got his rejection letter. He couldn't afford to go to a mental health center to get confirmation of the diagnosis I had given him. His mother assumed I was the one that made the decision to deny him benefits. The decision-making is actually done by doctors in the State capital. She didn't care. Her son was dead because the system failed.

Then there are those like Alphonso, who felt overwhelmed by the prospect of having to survive in this difficult world, and committed another crime so he could go back to the predictability of prison where there is a bed and three meals a day. The system sets people up for failure. They can't get jobs with their prison records and their driver's licenses have frequently been suspended so in places without public transportation they can't get to work even if they could get a job. Alphonso told me he was planning to wait until the weather got cold. Then he'd commit a crime that would get him about three months in prison. He could handle living on the streets when the weather was warm. He didn't like staying in shelters. He said there was too much crime there – more apparently than in prison. He slept in the woods when the weather was warm.

Melissa was ticketed for driving without her license. She was going to the park to run and left her purse at home. She didn't have the money to pay the ticket and didn't receive her court notice because she was evicted from her apartment. She ended up under arrest because she failed to appear in court.

Sarah and Joan were both arrested for forgetting to get a new sticker for their license plate. Do we not have better things to do with our tax dollars than to clog the courts with these kinds of cases?

Can't we just send them a reminder letter, attach their paycheck, or take it from their tax return if they don't pay up? I'm inclined to think most people will get that sticker with a reminder.

Jim missed a court-ordered class to take his mother to the hospital when she had a heart attack. He was given five more years on probation and an $8,000 fine, which seems a little excessive considering the crime. If he is unable to pay that fine at the end of five years, he will go to prison.

Jenny was arrested after calling the police when her husband slapped her so hard that she was sent flying into the wall. She had scratched her husband while trying to protect herself. The police said they had to arrest both of them since they both had injuries.

John was put in jail for seven months for driving without his glasses. This has to be a joke, right? Do we really want to put someone in jail for this – or any other traffic violation? We ruin his job prospects with a criminal record because he forgot his glasses? Who exactly is benefiting from John's misfortune and why are we letting them?

My understanding of the shortcomings of our prison system has not just been furthered by the prisoners I see after they get out of prison; I see the prison guards as well. They get injured in the line of duty or become too nervous to continue at their jobs, and apply for disability. Many regret ever having worked in prison. They feel the environment changes them; they become cynical and mean.

Jack was a former prison guard, who was angry that he had been made to stay in his maximum security job for four years. He was unable to take the stress and quit. He said that he was only supposed to be in that job for two years. They were supposed to rotate him out to an easier duty after that. He thought they kept him there because of his creative writing skills. He said he worked the night shift and could invent good excuses as to why the inmates were beaten when they came in at night. Inmates apparently are routinely met with a beating.

Amy was a former prison guard with Posttraumatic Stress Disorder. She was having nightmares of viewing an inmate with AIDS raping other prisoners. Apparently the guards on that wing found it amusing to put the inmate with AIDS in the showers with other inmates they felt needed to be punished, and watch him attack and infect them.

Mel was a retired corrections officer who came in with his wife, who was applying for disability. He said that he buried toxic waste and needles in shallow holes on the grounds of the prison adjacent to the one where I worked. Oh great! It's not just the treatment-resistant parasites I got from prison water, but all the toxic waste seeping into the water supply that I was exposed to. Who knows what that stuff has done to me!

The Department of Juvenile Justice employees who shared my office had their own knowledge of corruption in the system. One of the juvenile probation officers, Rasheed, told me that he had a friend who had worked at a prison, and had been obligated to make donations to unspecified causes. He was told he would be *punished* if he did not donate, so he complied. He found out later when the warden lost his job that it was the warden collecting money for his own use. Apparently, the warden also had a cleaning company on the side that used prison supplies to operate, and was busted for that.

Rasheed had once worked at a prison drug treatment program, where an inmate he was working with seemed to always be smoking marijuana. Determined to find out where the inmate was getting his seemingly unending supply, Rasheed started asking around. He was quickly advised that he "did not want to know" and that he should stop asking or he would end up arrested for a stash that would mysteriously show up in his desk. It turned out that "marijuana sales" was his warden's side business.

I told Rasheed that I had a number of people come in for evaluation, who had their children placed with known sex offenders and wondered if he knew of a judge who might be involved in this. He did not, but said that in the county where I live, judges send juveniles to live with any relative they might have out of the county. They just don't want problem children there. He said when he used to work my county that he knew judges to put kids on a bus out of State if they had no relatives outside the county, leaving them to fend for themselves.

It's not only problems with the corrections system that have become even more evident working in my current job. I have seen countless other people who worked all their lives and lost their health insurance after having an accident or illness which kept them from working. If worker's comp will help at all, they often delay treatment so long that the injury which could have been repaired becomes a permanent disability. People often lose their homes before they can qualify for assistance from social security disability.

I have also seen many children applying for disability for minor learning problems or ADHD. Granting children disability payments has resulted in horrific abuse of children with parents scamming the system at their children's expense. Many children without disabilities are put on medication unnecessarily when they are perhaps bored or daydreaming in class because if they are diagnosed with ADHD they will qualify for disability payments. Parents may hold back children in school even though they can keep up with the work, saying that the child is too immature to go ahead so later on paper it looks like the child had a history of learning problems. I've seen many children who were denied glasses or hearing aids so they would do poorly in school and qualify for disability. Do we wonder why these children grow up to be angry adults?

I had one young boy tell me that he was tired of people thinking he was stupid. I told him that the solution to that was to stop acting like he was stupid. (It was apparent from his testing that he was not putting forth consistent effort; i.e., he was faking). I saw his grandmother a couple of months later when she brought in his sister for an evaluation. She said a "miracle" happened when her grandson left my office. He was suddenly able to read and complete his other school work. He was being placed in a regular classroom.

Many of the children I see for learning disabilities testing need glasses, but either have never been prescribed the glasses they need, outgrew the glasses they have, or lost or broke the glasses they once had. According to a school psychologist I know, the children she tested for learning problems always had their vision tested. Then why didn't they get referrals? Parents have told me their child's pediatrician refuses to give them a referral even though the parent has observed the child reading with the book very close to his or her face.

In addition to needing glasses to magnify what they read, many of the children I see have perceptual distortions as well. Letters are reversed in their visual field so that "b's" look like "d's." Letters may also be transposed so that they see the word "was" as "saw." Often, looking through a colored plastic sheet to read can correct that distortion. Colored lenses or prisms can be put into their glasses as well. For most children I see, light blue works best to correct the distortion.

Recent studies have shown that the overuse of antibiotics, as well as hormones, including birth control pills, and any variety of other medications, have killed off much of the good bacteria in the mothers of these children. Birth by C-section and feeding with formula rather than breast milk further lower the infant's supply of good bacteria. Much of the increase in these learning problems as well as ADHD, autism, seizure disorders, depression, anxiety, psychosis, and associated physical disorders such as allergies, asthma, skin disorders, and stomach problems may stem from leaky gut which results from a low good bacteria count. Supplementation with probiotics and diets like the GAPS (Gut and Psychology Syndrome) diet can help to correct these problems. Iodine deficiency may also be a factor in these problems.

GMO crops are also adversely affecting our guts. GMO corn is engineered to be pesticide resistant, and the heavy chemical pesticides they are sprayed with poke holes in the intestines causing leaky gut. GMO corn has also been shown to cause tumors in rats and diminish their life span. Russia has outlawed the importation of GMO corn, but our government protects the wealthy who poison us.

More often than not, the children I see come in for testing without eating breakfast or having eaten only sugary cereal even though I specify to the parent that they should eat a breakfast with protein and no sugar. A lot of children have undetected blood sugar problems which create "brain fog" when they miss a meal or load up on sugar. I always send them to eat a breakfast with some protein before I test them.

Disability payments are something working people receive when they are not capable of maintaining employment. Children are not of working age and should not be receiving disability payments. The only way to stop this abuse of children is to take away their disability payments.

A person who has been punished is not less inclined to behave in a given way; at best, he learns how to avoid punishment.

B.F. Skinner

If people are good only because they fear punishment and hope for reward, then we are a sorry lot indeed.

Albert Einstein

Chapter IV

Connecting the Dots
The Punishers

A bright young man came in to my office not long after I left the prison system. His health problems were complicated by living in a small town, fundamentalist culture. He mentioned to some people at his church that he believed in evolution, and he feels he has been *punished* since. He was conscious that many of the people in his town devalue education and that the fact that he has had a few years of college is enough to make him suspect. He felt that everyone in his small community knew that he believed in science and that people in the street glared at him. They made fun of him because he "wasted" years of his life in college. Salvation comes from church membership and accepting Jesus as their savior. Any other pursuits in life are wasted. People who think differently should be *punished*. I suggest that he might want to move to the city.

The word *"punish"* was key to solving this puzzle. *"Punish"* resonated loud and clear – a moral judgment had been made. This was no different from the behavior of the prison guards, who apparently felt it their duty to punish both prisoners and women working at the prisons.

This young man's experience confirmed that my beliefs regarding science likely contributed to my harassment as well. My clerk at the prison reception center had become very upset when I told her that I believed in evolution, saying that I could not be a Christian if I believed in science. I told her that I did not find Christianity and evolution incompatible, but she did not agree, and remained quite upset. I knew that as a divorced woman, I was not accepted in this primitive Christian prison culture. Believing in science may be an even worse sin. How can this ignorance still prevail in this day and age?

Being an outsider of this religious club may be enough to rank me as a target for punishment. While I had thought security at the prisons harassed me because I was a mental health worker, it seems my spiritual beliefs may have been even more offensive to them. It has never made sense to me that only those who accept Christ as their savior will be saved. What about people born in countries where Buddhism or Islam are the primary religions? A sane god could not possibly punish people because of where they were born! Yet these fundamentalists insist that regardless of where they were born, righteous people would have found their way to Christ, and that all the people who don't will certainly end up in hell. I guess if you view your God as insanely punishing, it would follow that you could believe this. How glad I am that I was brought up in churches that believed in a loving, forgiving, sane God!

Rasheed, one of the juvenile probation officers at my office, told me that even his co-workers who have college degrees do not believe in evolution and say a prayer before their work meetings. He said that he is supposed to put in his reports to the judge whether or not the kids he works with are attending church. He refuses to do so. Are these Florida judges using religious affiliation to determine sentences?

I started researching these strange religious beliefs that they called "Christian." I looked up the Southern Baptist Church on the internet and saw that President Jimmy Carter left the church because of the belief that women should be subservient to men and that the Bible can only be interpreted by the minister. Some of the pieces are starting to fit together.

During this time, I met a former high ranking security officer from the prison, who told me that the Department of Corrections "conspires" against certain people. He did not specifically say that I was being targeted, but thought I should know about this. I could be on their list.

Shortly after I moved onto my land, the in-laws of my former clerk at the reception center moved in next to me. When I was late leaving for work one day, I saw a truck load of prisoners working in their yard. The prisoners quickly jumped in the truck and left after they saw me watching them. How did my neighbor rate this service? I was told he had retired from a prison maintenance job in Orlando – not exactly a high ranking position. Prisoners were not supposed to be working for private citizens anyway. A prison locksmith moved in on the other side of my house. During the construction of my home, several white prison cars gathered at these homes next to mine on a regular basis. After I took pictures of them, they apparently found somewhere else to meet.

I had a sex offender come in to apply for social security, who said he had moved to Interlachen, a town in the northern part of the state, because no one checks on sex offenders there. When he lived in a larger, nearby city, he had a probation officer checking on him at his home every month, but no one seems to care in this small town. However, he said he has a loud ringing noise in his home, similar to the one in my office. Are we both being bugged? I've got that noise at home too!

In the next few years after I left my prison job, I met other mental health workers who had been fired or run out of their jobs as I had been. A psychiatrist, Louise, had worked at the same reception center as I did. Like me, she was told she was taking too long in interviewing the inmates. And like I did, she told them that, ethically, she had to do a proper job in order to make a valid diagnosis and treat the inmates appropriately. She often stayed after hours to complete her paperwork, and security had suggested she must have been staying late because she was having an affair with an inmate. She had inherited some of my problem workers at that prison. She knew about the weekly prayer meetings, and also felt they were actually strategy meetings to plan ways to get rid of people who presented problems to their corrupt system.

Louise felt that outsiders don't understand the challenge of working in a corrupt system and the offense taken by those steeped in corruption when you won't join them. To defend inmates is a cardinal sin in the prison system, and those who want to help inmates are seen as traitors. Family and friends think you must be the difficult one not to fit in the system. Louise used the word "evil" to describe the people who bullied her. Like in my own experience, Louise said she had never been so aware of the pervasiveness of evil until she moved to North Florida and worked in the prison system. And like most mental health workers, it wasn't primarily the inmates she saw as evil, but the corrections officers. She laughed when I told her I referred to the county where I live as "Hell, Florida." She also worked with the clerk who caused me so many problems and found her attitude and behavior with inmates to be intolerable. She was stunned that this clerk's in-laws moved next to me and that my harassment continued after I left my prison job. She suggested that anyone considering a prison job should read "Lord of the Flies" because this is the level at which prison workers function.

I told Louise of a book I was reading by Harry Van Gelder called *Inner Peace Through the Process of Knowing*. He said that an honest person will find herself very alone in the world with most people working against her since most people in the world resent honesty. Few people even recognize the corruption that pervades our society, and those who do are scorned as disloyal to the system. The biggest value in our society is not the freedom and individualism we say that this country stands for, but conformity and loyalty to the status quo. Those people who think and question the status quo are seen as traitors.

Louise was having chest pains and difficulty breathing after walking off her prison job. She had been fearful her co-workers were trying to set her up and that she might lose her license if she stayed on the job. We talked of ways of finding peace even within the prevailing chaos and corruption of our society. I feel lucky that I'm working independently and am not pushed to compromise the care I give the people I evaluate. I may be scheduled for a 45 minute evaluation, but I can spend an hour and a half if that's what it takes to get all the information I need. My satisfaction has never come from the money I make.

Louise also noticed that a person's job position had little to do with their power in prison. Our common clerk seemed to have huge power in this organization even at her lowly position. There's got to be some other organization that gives people their status here.

Louise ended up taking another prison job. She has a family to support. Regrettably, I know that being a person of integrity,

79

committed to the ethical treatment of her inmate patients, Louise will likely continue to have problems working for the State of Florida.

I met a psychological specialist, Greta, at a party. She worked at a women's prison, and was upset at the way security treats the young women. She said they like to taunt the young inmates to the point of losing it so they can get some physical contact as they restrain them. They told one pretty young woman that they knew where her mother lived and were going to pay her a visit one evening. Her mother lived alone and the young girl became hysterical. The officers groped her as they restrained and handcuffed her.

Dina also worked as a psychological specialist at a prison. She tried for three months to get permission for an inmate to talk with his dying father. When the nursing home called saying there was no time to wait, she made a clinical decision to allow the inmate to talk to his father. She was fired because she had allowed the inmate to talk on her phone. She was granted unemployment after a hearing, but did not attempt to get back her job or sue the state. She said she was afraid they might burn down her home.

I later met Shelley, a psychologist who was fired years ago at a nearby prison. She was one of the earlier female psychologists to be employed in a Florida prison. She said that she was routinely left alone with inmates and was almost raped on one occasion. One of her male psych. specialists happened to walk by and pulled the inmate off her as he held a pen to her neck. Although she stayed in her job after her close call, the system soon found another way to get rid of her.

Shelley's daughter had married into a primitive Christian cult. That church never held weddings in their own building. Everyone took the pastor to other churches that would rent to them or got married at the court house and later had a private religious ceremony at home. Do they not want the notice in the newspaper to identify them with their own church? Do they not want their friends to know their fundamentalist orientation? Why are these people in hiding?

Shelley said that her daughter became compulsive about exercising while in that marriage. She had to work-out two hours a day to maintain her weight to please her husband, and would become very anxious if she had to miss a work-out. Her husband didn't want her to work and her job was to stay beautiful.

After Shelley's daughter separated from her husband, she was told that she would owe the entire church an apology when she went back to him. She didn't go back and is now happily remarried.

I continued to find doors closed to me for no apparent reason after I left my prison job. My friend, Brenda, wanted to get a reading and I took her to a spiritual church in Jacksonville for her birthday. Although there were only four cars in the parking lot and three of the four psychics in the room were sitting without customers, a woman came up and told us they were booked all day. People were waiting in the back of the church for their turn – we just couldn't see them. Or their invisible cars? A church was turning us away – and obviously lying to us? What is going on here? I later met another psychic from that church, who told me this was actually a fundamentalist, "conservative Republican" church. How can they be fundamentalist, Republican, and psychic at the same time? I guess in the South anything's possible. Maybe I was on their list too. Is their list and the prison list one and the same? Is it a Republican list or a fundamentalist list? Is there a difference?

I had written a children's football book years ago, but never seemed to be able to find anyone to illustrate it. I went to a local college art class to see if anyone was interested in illustrating the book. I told the instructor that I knew someone who could get several well-known college and pro football coaches to endorse the book. Amazingly enough, the instructor told me none of the students were interested in a summer job illustrating the book. I phoned the local university and tried to get an ad in their employment listing, but the ad never appeared. Is all of this just coincidence?

Let the one among you who is without sin be the first to cast a stone.

Jesus

Chapter V

The Christian Taliban

Two books were very helpful in understanding what was going on in my life: *The Good News Club* by Katherine Stewart and *Quiverfull* by Kathryn Joyce. According to Katherine Stewart, most fundamentalists believe that the Bible is the literal word of God, that finding their way into the right kind of Christianity is the only path to salvation, and that they are involved in a daily struggle with Satan.

This pseudo-Christian movement likes to call itself the Patriarchy movement, but in effect they are just another form of the Muslim Taliban. There is a civil war going on in this country that the Christian Taliban apparently hopes to export to the rest of the world. I've been told of people in my area, who homeschool their children and spend the day practicing military drills with them. They apparently model themselves on the Muslim Taliban. Was it the American soldiers in Desert Storm who fueled this movement after being taunted by Muslims about not being able to control their women?

There are racial and political tones to this movement as the Christian Taliban feels Whites need to have more children to keep up with minority birth rates as well as boost the rolls of Republicans to further their agenda. For the first time in 2012, there were more minority births in this country than White births. In Europe, there is a fear that Muslims are reproducing at a much faster rate than White Christians, and in Poland, in particular, a woman may be seen as unpatriotic if she does not have as many children as she is capable of having. The Christian Identity organization, which reportedly has a branch in Tampa, is an Aryan Nation affiliate.

Unfortunately, this is a covert war of which most people are unaware. Like the Muslim Taliban, the Christian Taliban uses the pretense of knowing God's will, which they feel justified in imposing on the rest of the world. They want a new society in which women will again be subservient to and dependent upon men, yet responsible for everything that goes wrong even when they don't make the decisions. If their husbands fail in their businesses, it's because their wives were not sufficiently supportive. However, if their wives help them succeed, the men take credit for everything that goes right. A man should also get credit for anything good his wife or daughter does because he has influenced her to do it. If the man beats his wife, it's because the woman has provoked him. Everything women fought to escape in the last century is being brought back in full force. Women and children would again be the property of their fathers and then their husbands. Daughters would be sold by their fathers to the highest bidder. Women may not be able to own property in this new world. When I was being ripped off by contractor after contractor while building my house, a retired prison warden who lives nearby asked me, "What do you expect when you're a woman building a house alone?"

I had friends whose pretty teenage daughter, Christina, was arrested for shoplifting, but the charges were dropped. The arresting officer told her father that they were letting her off because she was a good student. The two other teens arrested with her were not so fortunate. Christina shortly after confided to her parents that she had lost her virginity to a stranger in the parking lot of the store where she worked. She said he was just some random guy who walked into the store and asked her to meet him in the parking lot. A juvenile justice worker told me that it is common for young girls in this area to have their charges dropped in return for submitting sexually to the male authorities. I suspected this was the real story behind what happened with my friends' daughter. I also had a man come for a social security evaluation, who said his girlfriend got her charges dropped by submitting sexually to the deputy. Submission is apparently redeeming in their scheme of things. Does having sex with the cop make them good Christians? Is this what a theocracy is all about?

There was a time when the feudal lords were entitled to the virginity of those they governed. Maybe these guys think they should have that right as well.

In *Quiverfull,* Kathryn Joyce points out that the women of this movement voluntarily "de-self," giving up their own identity and power over their lives for what they have been brainwashed to believe is the higher good and God's will.

They are told that upon the Second Coming, they will be the rulers, and the feminists and other nonbelievers will be their slaves. In effect there would be a caste system where nonbelievers would be second class citizens, undeserving of respect or even of government services.

While they label more liberal religions "humanist" and criticize them for what they see as the relativity of their values, the Christian Taliban readily compartmentalizes their own values and are full ready to compromise the Ten Commandments. They believe abortion is murder, but killing people during a war is noble. The compartmentalization is especially prevalent when dealing with women who dare not to submit to the rule of men.

Single women have no status in their world. A woman's status comes from her father and then her husband. An unwed woman is a source of temptation and refusal to marry is viewed as rebellion. Independent women have to be *punished* to be brought into line, and it's fully appropriate to make an example of them for other women by stealing from them, deceiving them, harassing and making fun of them, and trying to sabotage their work. The men control the women in their lives by making it appear to be dangerous in the outside world without a man in their lives to protect them.

Having control over the women in their lives gives men the illusion that they are in control of their own lives. They don't recognize the control they have given up to the pseudo-religion.

They say that women can be easily deceived and because of this, men are smarter and need to be in charge. They don't get that the ability to con people is not proof of being smarter than the people conned. It is only proof of their lack of morality.

After I started researching these primitive cults, I gained new insight as to problems I had been having in my life for years. I once supervised a Southern Baptist student who refused to make the revisions I had made to his reports. It was not just that he had issues with authority in general. I now can see that he likely was refusing to be supervised by a woman – refusing to acknowledge her expertise and follow her direction because of his religious beliefs.

Several years ago, I worked in the same office with a man who told me he went to a "Titan" workshop to treat his anxiety. I had never heard of Titan training at this time, but I now know that this man was likely not attending any kind of mental health workshop, but a fundamentalist workshop. He was being told that it was women in the modern world who were responsible for his anxiety because they emasculated him with their success. Forcing women to stay in their place was the way to lower his anxiety.

The construction workers who played Christian music all day long while working on my house, but intentionally messed up and stole from me, perhaps thought they'd be rewarded in heaven for giving me a hard time. Or perhaps they had no conscience to start with and found a convenient religion to allow them to exercise that lack of conscience. In any case, the Ten Commandments do not have to be followed with people outside the cult.

The Christian Taliban movement could even be construed as an Anti-Christ movement. They call themselves Christian, but are making a mockery of all that is good in the Christian faith. They are poisoning the minds of children and stealing them from unsuspecting parents. In the field of psychology people without conscience are labeled "antisocial." This movement is an "antisocial" movement – one in which people who are kind to others are mocked. People who treat outsiders badly are considered the best of Christians. The teachings of Jesus have been distorted to the point that they are opposite to what Jesus actually said. "Love your neighbor" does not apply unless your neighbor submits to the Christian Taliban law.

In her book, *Quiverfull,* Kathryn Joyce points out that some of these pseudo-Christians believe women who get divorced should get the death penalty - not men who divorce, mind you, just women. Men do no wrong in this scheme of things (unless of course they happen to be LGBT, and are condemned to death right along with divorced women). Some apparently believe a woman can only show true repentance by committing suicide.

In this distorted belief system, husbands and fathers are representatives of the divine. For a woman to disobey a man is equivalent to disobeying God. Rebellion is seen as the sin of witchcraft, and witchcraft is also punishable by death. Are these people living in the real world? Of the fifty-five major prisons in Florida only four are for women. According to the Florida Department of Corrections website, 93% of prisoners in Florida are men. The physical and sexual abuse of children and women is largely the work of men. How exactly can they conceive of men as having a better moral compass than women?

Dr. Daniel Amen, who has had many PBS programs on the brain, has compared the brains of tens of thousands of men and women, and has found women to be much better suited to making decisions due to their superior intuition, impulse control, empathy, and ability to cooperate.

I often see morally challenged young men coming in for social security reevaluations at the age of eighteen. They already have a long history of trouble with the law. Mothers know their sons have more difficulty staying on the right side of the law than their daughters. Often it is a girlfriend who is able to help young men make better decisions, and I frequently suggest to these young men that due to their proven poor decision-making skills, they would do well to defer to their girlfriends' better sense. They laugh because they know what I'm saying is true.

According to the Taliban, an obedient woman should learn how not to upset her husband. A "godly" woman can improve her husband's behavior through submission. She should keep his flaws hidden. A woman can be punished in a fundamentalist church for asking the minister for help with her abusive husband because she should not be revealing any flaws her husband might have. Women should be the keepers of family secrets. The State of Florida shows its theocratic bent when women are arrested for reporting husbands who beat them.

A woman is to be sexually available at all times for all activities. I know a woman who became pregnant when her husband initiated sex with her in her sleep. I guess the idea of being able to consent is irrelevant when you have to be available at any time. There can be no rape by a husband in this scheme of things.

According to certain Christian Taliban sects, women should not learn career skills even as emergency backups to support themselves as this can teach girls attitudes of independence. They must prepare to marry and "conduct war on the home front." They shouldn't waste time with college, work, or missions. It wasn't just ignorance that made prison security call me "Mrs. Humphreys" rather than "Dr. Humphreys." The education of women to a "man's level" is not recognized by this cult.

For sects that allow college for women, the goal should be to catch a good husband or to train in roles to support men. If they go to college, it should be close to home so that the father can look after them and assure they remain pure.

Christian Taliban families believe the father should be the provider and breadwinner, yet women are encouraged to start home businesses to make the family self-supporting. So while it is stated that women's only purpose is having and raising children, and they are encouraged to stay home and have ten children, they are expected to bring in their share of income from home while already overly burdened by raising ten children. This is just another of their contradictions.

The fundamentalists preach that women should be respectful of all men, judging carefully whether they should even speak in mixed company. After all, when she speaks, a man does not have the opportunity to speak (and women have nothing important to say?). Women cannot speak at all in some churches; they have to rely on men to say anything.

Women should not hang around other women who might influence them against their husbands or their church. I had a friend from college who quit phoning me several years ago. She would be ever so happy to hear from me, but never initiated contact herself. My friend is a Southern Baptist. She hasn't phoned me since I stopped calling her. She wrote me a note on a Christmas card a couple of years ago, saying she wanted to see me, but I figured I'd wait and see if she called. *I'm still waiting.* I've since had other so- called Christian friends follow the same pattern. Some even claim they can't bring themselves to make phone calls – like they have some sort of psychological problem. Strange how they can use that phone at work.

Women of this cult may also insist on bringing their husbands with them when they meet with a nonmember so that he can protect her from the influence of a "Jezebel."

According to this movement, women should not be allowed in any positions where they would supervise men. Girls should be trained from an early age to defer to their brothers. Some of my male supervisees in my prison jobs openly refused to follow my direction with little or no consequence.

There's also a trend toward "covenant marriages" making it more difficult to divorce. The pre-nup or contract with the father can delineate who the couple can associate with. While unaware family members may think a pre-nup is about finances, it can actually be barring them from the young couple's lives if they are not members of the right religious club. If the parents are not members, they may not even be allowed to know of the "covenant," leaving them confused as to why they are being excluded from their child's life. The child will concoct some story which blames the parents for their estrangement. Often it can be something so obviously false that the parent may think their child delusional.

Fundamentalists believe that no fault divorce and contraception programs should be repealed, tax breaks should be given to large families, and there should be different pay for men and women with men, of course, getting paid much better for the same job because it is their role to support the family. Why exactly are there so many single women on AFDC if men are supporting the children?

The Christian Taliban Patriarchy movement has openly declared a "War on our Culture," which they equate with Satan. This could just as well be labelled a "War on Women." Yet our government is not responding to this threat. What is going on in this country?

I looked toward our government to protect me, but our government has failed me. I went to just about every level of law enforcement, including the FBI and Homeland Security, and wrote two governors and the president. Interestingly enough, when I went to the FBI, I told them I suspected that my computer was being monitored. Since I had confidential federal information on my computer, I thought they might check it out for me. I was told that they didn't have the capacity to work with computers and that I might want to try the Geek Squad at Best Buy! The FBI doesn't work with computers? Really???

I also appealed to several attorneys to help me, but no one apparently wanted to face the consequences of confronting the Taliban - or perhaps they all belonged to the Taliban. I actually called another local attorney's office (he did not handle lawsuits) to find out who might be able to check for bugs in my office, computer, home etc., and was told I would need to go out of this state to get someone honest. Then I decided I would just hire an investigator myself, but again struck out. One investigator told me he would only work with me if I had an attorney.

I have been the brunt of religious harassment and persecution in my workplace and in my home. While their leaders and those attending their conferences are vocal in their beliefs, the Christian Taliban trains many others to hide their affiliation from those they persecute - perhaps so they cannot be convicted of hate crimes. They often marry in churches other than their own or in civil ceremonies so their affiliation cannot be traced. They rewrite their histories to be consistent with their beliefs.

Of course, children recruited into this nonsense do not let their families know the motivation for their often bizarre behavior. They are likely to reject family for no apparent reason and project the blame onto them. This is part of their psychological warfare. I have come to know that many people in this cult routinely lie about their religion. Security officers in prison said they disliked mental health when it was really the more liberal religious beliefs of most mental health workers (and their marital status) that they felt needed to be punished.

The lot of divorced or never-married single mothers is particularly cruel if their children are recruited to the Taliban. Since converts believe that a home without a man in it is not a Christian home, they may refuse to visit their mothers at all in their homes or allow their grandchildren to visit them. They are committed to punishing the divorced woman for what the cult has told them are their mother's sins. Like most abusers, they seek to isolate the women they target so they will be totally alone in the world.

Single parents may suffer for years, not knowing that their children have a religious psychosis that makes them want to punish their divorced mother. Undoubtedly, the adult children can gloat in what this cult would view as their mother's stupidity in taking so long to accept that her children could intentionally try to hurt her.

But it is not just single parents who suffer this type of rejection. A couple I know was totally shut out of their daughter's life, because they were outside the cult. They had let the grandparents take their daughter to a fundamentalist church, and as soon as she turned eighteen, she moved out (into a *deputy sheriff's* home temporarily and then with her grandparents) and refused to have anything to do with her parents. Her parents were totally grief stricken, but eventually figured out they would have to join the Taliban to be accepted by their daughter and having done so, now have her back in their lives.

Other nonmember parents have complained to me that the fundamentalist grandparents blatantly favor their siblings' children who attend their church over their own children. The sibling's children are taken out for their birthdays and frequently spend the night with the grandparents while their own children are ignored. The nonmember parents typically have no idea why their children are being discriminated against by the grandparents and the grandparents will not tell them.

The fundamentalists believe that the purpose of discipline is to show "love" to the unrepentant, restoring the sinner to right relation with Christ. This might explain why prison guards think it their job to punish the inmates. Abuse equals love by their definition. Of course, they do not believe they even need to tell people what their beliefs are because if they are righteous people, they'll be magically led to Christ via the right church.

Part of the appeal of this sort of religion is that people can have status in the eyes of the church when they have none in the world outside. They can feel superior to their doctors, lawyers, and anyone else with education, because status in the world outside the church doesn't count. So they can scorn the silly people who spend their time and money seeking education, because all that is meaningless in their scheme of things. They believe they are right in punishing people outside the cult by cheating, lying, and excluding them, because anyone not "saved" by their definition of "saved" is evil and deserves punishment.

I see this movement as a "cult" even though it does not have one leader, like Jim Jones, that they are blindly following as we typically think of in a cult. In this case it is the doctrine coming from the leadership of their churches that they follow blindly. They also see everyone that does not believe their doctrine as evil enemies, and see themselves as superior to anyone who disagrees with them. As in a cult, there is no tolerance of dissent with punishment applied to those who dare deviate from their rigid beliefs.

I have met women who were the victims of what some might call "medical errors." Yet I wonder due to the bizarre nature of some of these errors whether they were errors or intentional punishment of wayward women. One woman, who was divorcing her fundamentalist husband, received radiation treatment for cervical cancer which burned her intestines so badly that they had to be removed. How do you miss by location and intensity to that degree? Was that really just carelessness? She was left with chronic pain and an external bag to replace her intestines. When I saw her, she said that she had seen the error of her ways. She was thinking she should return to her husband and his church. Had she been told that her misfortune was God's way of punishing her for leaving her husband?

Another woman told me that a pelvic bone had not returned to normal position following childbirth, and her doctor's solution was to remove the bone. Apparently this bone is essential to stabilize the hips and should never be removed. She spoke with a number of attorneys who refused to take her case even though other doctors later told her this surgery was a travesty. The doctor who performed the surgery was apparently a well-respected doctor at a teaching hospital. I can only wonder whether she was being intentionally punished. She only had two children. Was that her sin? Had she been divorced?

A pretty young woman told me that after leaving her in labor for more than 30 hours, her doctor had given her a sideways episiotomy, cutting into her muscle. This made her recovery from childbirth particularly painful and prolonged. As with the woman with the pelvic bone removed, her subsequent doctors were appalled that this had been done to her. They said that this is never done and could not fathom why this doctor would cause her such pain. Was this woman being punished for something? She had used birth control for years before she had her first child. Was that her sin? Is it "fear" keeping people in this bizarre cult?

My elderly father lived in Jacksonville before his death at the age of 91, and I visited him frequently on weekends. Whenever I spent the night at my father's home after I left the prison job, air was let out of at least one of my tires. It became routine to get out my father's compressor before I left and fill up my tires. They didn't flatten my tires. They just let out about ten pounds of pressure – enough to be dangerous for a Ford Explorer. I took my car to Firestone to get the tires checked and they said there were no leaks. Even after I got the tires replaced with new ones, I continued to lose air overnight whenever I stayed at my father's house – and nowhere else. This continued for a couple of years until I noticed one day when I was getting on the internet while visiting my father that along with my Verizon and other neighbors' netgear etc., there was a listing for *"Infidel Info Network."* I clicked there and was told either to hit some sort of key I couldn't identify or to enter my password. After I pointed this out to my father, the site disappeared and my tires no longer lost air when I spent the night. I don't think Muslims would be so bold as to have an internet listing by that name, but the pseudo-Christians in this area could easily get away with it.

This makes me wonder whether this organization has a targeted list of offending women, available to all its members. Do we have to check a doctor's religious affiliation before we get medical care these days? I don't think there's any way of reliably doing that. How about nurses in hospitals or nursing homes? Maybe we need to compile a new sort of "Angie's List" for doctors and other trustworthy professionals who are not fundamentalists seeking to punish anyone who disagrees with their beliefs.

In her book, *The Good News Club,* Katherine Stewart points out that this is a stealth movement, which attempts to work invisibly to turn children against any rational parent. They are rewriting our history, saying that the US was founded as a "Christian nation," rather than a nation founded on "religious freedom." They proclaim that it is the right of Christians to take back the country.

Other than the "Good News Clubs" that our Supreme Court has allowed to infiltrate our schools and brainwash our children, there are a number of other groups that disguise themselves as nondenominational or as giving nonreligious morality classes. These groups may carry titles like Teen Mania and Battle Cry, and often use bullying to get children to join them. Of course, there are a variety of Christian athletic groups also furthering the cause. Homeschooled Tim Tebow, who was unable to translate his high school success onto the professional football field, seems to be revered by these Christians and has had unusual staying power in the sports industry after successive failures.

The Michigan Senate actually passed a measure on bullying that included an *exemption* for anyone who bullies out of *sincerely held religious belief or moral conviction.* The exemption was fortunately deleted due to a widespread outcry by those not belonging to this cultish religious movement.

These are not uncoordinated efforts by individual sects. There are a long list of interdenominational groups pursuing the goal of subjugating women and making this a patriarchal nation. You can find these groups listed in both Katherine Stewart's and Kathryn Joyce's books. The Republican Party represents them.

So how can we know who these people are to protect our children from them? Many *Taliban* families have home churches as none around are strict enough for them. If they do attend a fundamentalist church, they may keep this fact from others not associated with their church. Their target group is children 4-14, who are most easily brain-washed. Often Taliban parents homeschool their children, but some send them to public schools.

While there are interdenominational organizations pursuing the subjugation of women, the separate factions of this movement do not necessarily represent a homogenous group. While extremists believe in the necessity of promoting the White race by having a "quiverfull" of children, homeschooling their children, teaching their children military tactics for the "war against Satan," and establishing financially independent family units, the less extreme sects, who hold regular jobs and send their children to public schools are no less dangerous. Large numbers of these stealth warriors are hiding among the general population and recruiting new members from our children.

There is no sure way of knowing who all these people are, but a certain characteristic mode of operation seems to be universal. By virtue of being the "chosen," they also feel they are the "entitled." They feel that people outside the cult, especially women, do not deserve to have anything, especially money. These antisocial traits extend to trying to take your money any way they can, whether by wasting your food, destroying things you care about, or overcharging you for work. While they invite you to celebrate their birthdays, they will ignore yours or participate minimally in any celebration you have. There will be no reciprocating for anything you do for them; they don't feel you deserve it. This movement is all about power and control. Nonmembers may not be permitted by their fundamentalist families to host holiday dinners as they do not have the status of an adult and are not deemed worthy of that honor. In fact, they may not be allowed to participate in any family decisions, even as trivial as deciding what restaurant to meet at for dinner or what movie to watch. The 2nd class nonmembers are treated as children; they are welcome to tag along as long as they do not make any demands. Unmarried women need to accept their place as inferior not only to men, but to married women as well.

Parents outside the cult may find they must initiate every phone call to their children. Their children may put them on a group email list, letting their parents know they have no special status in their lives. If they stay in contact at all, the adult children will find many other ways of letting their parents know that they do not hold the place parents would expect to hold in their lives. They will make a point of "dishonoring" their parents. They may stay with other family members rather than their parents when they are in town – especially with any family members the parents do not get along with. Typically the children will expect the parents to act in the role of parent, paying for their college tuition and weddings, supporting them otherwise financially, and perhaps even babysitting the grandchildren at their children's homes (not their own), but these parents cannot expect their due as parents. When they need help, their adult children will be too busy to assist. These children expect their parents to fulfill their roles as parents, but do not feel they need to fulfill their roles as their children since their parents are outside the cult and therefore second class citizens who deserve nothing from them.

If the parent is so fortunate as to be able to visit their indoctrinated children's homes, they will likely be greeted by an empty refrigerator, which they will need to fill. They should not expect their children to actually cook for them, because the children see the nonmember parents as servants, who should be doing everything for them. If the parent offers to take them out for dinner, they will choose a place where they can run up the bill with expensive drinks, appetizers, and desserts. The children will take the parents' money anyway they can as they feel those who do not belong to their religion are undeserving and should suffer. Particularly undeserving are women who are not married; they should live in poverty. "Honor your mother" becomes "Punish your mother."

These fundamentalists are especially targeting children perceived as leaders in their schools. Parents should be particularly vigilant of school sports activities as these are recruiting grounds for the Taliban. Our laws regarding separation of church and state make it illegal for football coaches to pray before or after games, but this is routinely done in many high schools and colleges. It is also unlawful for coaches to take their teams to church, yet many college coaches routinely do this. Athletic groups that call themselves "Christian" are likely filled with these radicals. Parents should also be aware of extracurricular activities that teachers are giving extra credit for. These may be cult-sponsored events.

In hiring, fundamentalist businesses often will ask prospective employees whether they can work on Sundays, even if the business is closed on Sundays. If the applicant says she is available to work on Sundays, she will not be hired.

It is incumbent upon the women in this country to preserve our way of life. If we fail to do so, we are likely to return to an insane time where a new Inquisition engages in witch-hunting. The State of Florida is effectively an undeclared theocracy, where women outside the movement cannot get legal representation, where law enforcement abuses its power, and where doctors can commit crimes unpunished. I know the same must be happening largely undetected in other areas of the country.

Where are the sane Christian churches and why are they not doing more to counter the myths of the Taliban? I think it's time they took some leadership in protecting the good in the Christian religion. And where are the interfaith groups of sane religions, and why aren't they promoting peace, tolerance, and freedom for women?

I had a Muslim man come into my office not too long ago. He was very ill, but said he was not fearful of dying. He had lived a good life; he had treated all people with kindness. He knew that he was going to his reward for the good deeds he had done in life. The sane sects of all religions have in common that they are based on love and treating others with kindness. The punitive, fundamentalist branches of religions are based on fear, which translates into punishment of those who are different.

To hold onto our freedom, we must protect our children from the pseudo-Christians who would take them from us. We may know to warn our children about taking candy from strangers as they might be laced with drugs, but we also need to warn them about pseudo-Christians who might poison their minds. Advance warning is probably the best thing we can do to protect our children and ourselves so that we are not abandoned by children who learn to regard their parents as second class citizens who deserve punishment.

It is easier for a camel to go through the eye of a needle than it is for a rich man to enter the Kingdom of Heaven.

Jesus

The oppressed are allowed once every few years to decide which particular representatives of the oppressing class are to represent and repress them in parliament.

Vladimir Lenin

In our ecclesiastical region there are priests who don't baptize the children of single mothers because they weren't conceived in the sanctity of marriage. These are today's hypocrites.

Pope Francis

Patriotism is supporting your country all the time and your government when it deserves it.

Mark Twain

Chapter VI

The Development of Christian Fascism:

From Greed to Tyranny

There are a number of books that look at the development of this movement, among them, *The Family,* by Jeff Sharlett, *American Fascists* by Chris Hedges, and *Kingdom Coming* by Michelle Goldberg. These books show the captivation of the wealthy with the idea of their own God-appointed superiority and how this grew into a movement of the entitled seeking to dominate the world. When labor unions came into power, factory owners found it useful to take the counsel of religious leaders and claim the backing of Christ in their rule of their companies, eventually crushing unions and disabling the economy by sending manufacturing jobs overseas. Roosevelt's New Deal spurned reaction from the rich and powerful, who concluded that the poor need *nothing but Christ*. The physical needs of the poor were not important; only their souls needed to be nourished. In this vein Christianity was appropriated by a political movement, which has grown to support the selfish needs of the rich.

Fundamentalists promote the myth that it is women working and taking up men's jobs, which has caused our economic problems, diverting attention from the wealthy, who are actually responsible. Hence, the men feel justified in punishing and stealing from successful women, who they feel are responsible for their own struggles and who in their success have been robbing men of what might have been their own success.

While evangelicals now make up about 70 million Americans, reportedly only about 13% of the population (I believe this is an underestimate as many hide their beliefs) are the radical, Dominionist variety, who believe that these pseudo-Christians have a "God-given right to rule" and advocate replacing civil law with Old Testament biblical law (ignoring New Testament notions of forgiveness and tolerance). The move to post the Ten Commandments in courtrooms reflects this intent. That these fanatics are still relatively small in number is of little comfort; fascist movements historically have not needed large percentages of the population in their following to take over control of governments.

Goldberg calls the Dominionists "Christian Nationalists;" Chris Hedges calls them "American Fascists." These Christian terrorists may as well be called the "Christian Taliban" as they closely mimic the Muslim Taliban. This Taliban calls for a "stealth" penetration of secular institutions with the goal of transitioning to Christian rule.

According to the Christian Taliban, before Christ will grace us with his Second Coming, every part of our society must be made "Christian." In the Rapture, the "saved" will be lifted to heaven and the unsaved "left behind" to suffer a seven year period of torture and chaos known as the Tribulation. The popular Tim LaHaye *Left Behind* books and movies have helped the popularity of this notion.

Not only do these pseudo-Christians believe that they have been mandated by God to make the United States a Christian State, but they believe they have a sort of manifest destiny to extend their domination to the rest of the world – bringing forth a new age of American Imperialism. Anyone who disagrees with them is not deemed either Christian or patriotic.

Fascism was admired by some of the wealthy during the World War II era. Henry Ford even financed Hitler illegally. The problem fundamentalists now have with Hitler is not that he committed genocide, established a dictatorship, or spread his tyranny to other countries, but that he did not declare he was doing this for Jesus. Genocide can be established biblically by these fanatics, and any means of dominating the world for Jesus can be justified.

This movement would like a return to the days prior to the New Deal, replacing government welfare programs with private church charities where elitist pseudo-Christians would decide who deserves to be helped, and where that help may be contingent on their repentance and loyalty to the cause.

These pseudo-Christians are able to engage in acts of violence that are a violation of our generally held moral conventions, because in their view, the victims are responsible for their own suffering for having defied God. Bullying and other acts of violence against nonbelievers are encouraged. There is now a video game which gives teens practice in blowing away nonbelievers and the Army of the Antichrist.

Economic and political chaos is a friend to this movement. In the face of economic and social despair, people can hide in the fantasy that they are superior despite their limitations. And in this parallel universe, they are creating parallel "Christian" organizations to replace secular ones.

While they claim to be all about family, in fact, loyalty to God and church are placed above loyalty to family and friends, tearing apart families and communities. The church/political cell becomes the substitute for the extended family.

The movement creates paranoia with lies that it is the pseudo-Christians who are being persecuted by the liberal humanists, projecting their own agenda onto the rest of the world, and fueling more attacks on those who disagree with them. According to Americans United, Stanford University has started up a legal clinic to help "protect" the religious right from those who "persecute" them.

The Elite

In his books, *The Family* and *C-Street,* Jeff Sharlet, exposes an elite fundamentalist movement headquartered in Washington D.C. These elitists reportedly believe they have replaced the Jews as "God's chosen" to lead the world. They distance themselves from the populist movement which they consider a sort of "White trash" religion. However, according to Sharlet, they share with them the belief that they are superior to the rest of the world, and seek to establish the *rule* of Jesus. While the populists focus on domestic politics, the elite seek to manipulate world politics. Both groups label their political attempts to gain control "evangelism."

The elite have sought to separate religion from Christ. Sharlet says that family leader, Doug Coe, believes that religion distracts people from Jesus. According to Sharlet, the Family disapproves of any kind of ethics; in fact, ethics is seen as a *rule book for women*. Power, not morality, characterizes their God. They prefer to be called *Followers of Christ* rather than *Christians*. Doug Coe has reportedly gone so far as to say that it would be *irrelevant* if a man had raped three little girls. What counts is that the man is a *Follower of Christ* and loyal to The Family. Similarly, if a ruler of a nation they can benefit from commits genocide, that can be (and has been on a number of occasions) overlooked in the interest of their other goals. The Family has apparently influenced our foreign policy for years, repeatedly violating the Logan Act, which forbids private citizens from conducting diplomacy.

Like the populist movement, the Family apparently sees doing good works and helping the poor as irrelevant to salvation. Poverty is viewed as the result of disobedience, and thus the poor deserve their poverty. The only help the poor need is Jesus.

Sharlet says that the Family's goal is not to save souls as is characteristic of religious movements. Their goal is political - to rule the nation and the world at large. Democracy is seen as *rebelliousness,* and rights are seen as the product of an arrogant mind. A Worldwide Spiritual Offensive has been launched so that Jesus (in the guise of American power) can rule all countries.

The Family, reportedly modeling themselves after the communists, organize themselves in cells. Cell members monitor each other's lives with the cell having ultimate "veto rights" over each member's life. They commit to secrecy; the network must remain invisible. Doug Coe, leader of the elite, compares their invisibleness to the mafia. The National Prayer Breakfast, which has met each year in February since its establishment in 1953 and has been attended by our presidents, is their only publicized activity. At the yearly prayer breakfast non-Christians are welcomed to pray to the de-religioned Jesus.

Sharlet provides a long list of powerful people who have been affiliated with The Family, which has included even some

Democrats in their midst. Florida's long-time Democratic Senator Bill Nelson is reportedly a member, and surprisingly enough, Hillary Clinton attended a weekly Senate Prayer Breakfast. The Family is said to be backed by big money seeking to influence or bypass our government when necessary to get what they want. The Family's current headquarters was bought with money donated by arms manufacturer Raytheon.

The women of the elite have a separate house in Washington D.C. called "Potomac Point." Young "Christian" college women are required to dress "femininely" to serve the men at their male residences. It seems that like the populist movement, the elitists also place women in a supportive, subservient role. While the Family tries to separate themselves from popular fundamentalist notions of Christianity, Sharlet portrays the differences as slight and probably motivated by a desire to sway those leaders of countries with other religions to join them in their financial pursuits. The Family has reportedly bought its way into even Muslim nations and succeeded in setting up local Family groups with *Followers of Jesus* across the world.

A Different View

The boundaries between The Family and the populist fundamentalists are blurred in Sharlet's books with both seeming to have the same agenda. A quite different view of The Family can be obtained from former Congressman Mark Siljander's book, *A Deadly Misunderstanding*. Siljander is an admitted former fundamentalist and a current Family member, who believes the Bible has been mistranslated and misinterpreted, and that both fundamentalist Christians and Muslims distort the teachings of the Bible and the Qur'an. He points out numerous similarities between the two faiths. The core of both is that we love one another unconditionally – especially our enemies. The Qur'an, which actually mentions Jesus 110 times, says Jesus was uniquely righteous, pure and sinless.

Siljander believes that the word "convert" in the Bible was a mistranslation and that it actually refers to "surrender." Loving your neighbors is the essence of submitting to God's will because unconditional love is God's agenda. Jesus did not intend to start a new religion or send people out to "convert" the world to Christianity. He simply wanted people to treat each other with kindness and show love to their enemies.

Siljander notes that other major religions also include Jesus in their teachings. While Muslims see Jesus as a prophet, Hindus view him as one of the gods. Buddhists also revere Jesus. However, while Jesus is highly regarded by other religions, Christianity is not. Christianity is viewed as a racist excuse for American imperialism.

Gandhi is quoted as saying, "If Christians acted more like Jesus then I would be one."

The goals of the Muslim and Christian Talibans appear to be the same: to forge one gigantic deistic state under sharia or biblical law, transcending national boundaries and placing all infidels in subjugation.

To deal with fundamentalist Muslims, Siljander says that we must be organically decentralized ourselves, changing the movement by changing the ideology and showing them common ground. True religion is a state of being. Sijlander says he is not seeking conversion. The goal is reconciliation, resolution, and peace. He neglects to mention how to deal with American fundamentalists with the same agenda as the Muslim Taliban.

Siljander is critical of our government's approach to diplomacy. Rather than conflict resolution, the focus is on conflict containment. He states that the US State Department sees gestures toward personal friendship as signs of weakness. Negotiating with an enemy is a professional act; loving one's enemy is personal. Siljander says that our response to our worst enemies might be viewed as sulking; we simply refuse to talk to them at all. Rather than refusing to talk to our enemies, Siljander and The Family have been approaching even dictators who have committed genocide in an attempt to help them see our commonalities, and sway them toward "peace."

Mark Siljander went to prison for a year and a day in early 2012 for charges related to money laundering by a charitable organization he was affiliated with, and my efforts to contact him after his release failed. My mail to him was returned; there was no forwarding address. I then wrote Doug Coe at C-Street for clarification of the differences between fundamentalist beliefs and goals, and those of The Family, but did not hear back from him.

Progress Made by the Taliban

While still relatively small in number, this movement has largely gained control of the Republican Party, and has succeeded in tearing down the wall between church and state on a number of fronts. They are quickly infiltrating our government and our armed forces. Christian evangelicals now reportedly have more than 60% of chaplaincy appointments in the armed services and service academies, and use their position to openly proselytize cadets. The Christian Embassy organization reportedly holds weekly prayer meetings with about 40 generals.

Progress continues in the creation of parallel organizations as well. The Christian fundamentalists were reportedly involved in the building of Blackwater, a private security firm contracted with the US government, and its private intelligence branch called "Total Intelligence." This mercenary army paid for with government funds operates without constitutional constraint in our foreign wars.

There are numerous "Christian" lobbying groups and prayer groups representing the Christian Taliban in Washington, D.C. They have joined with Muslims in the UN to fight against international agreements protecting the rights of women and children.

President Bush created a White House office of Faith-Based and Community Initiatives, and set up similar offices in major government departments. While President Franklin D. Roosevelt had barred discrimination in government-funded programs, in 2001 Bush issued an executive rule allowing religious discrimination in federally funded hiring. It had already been established that churches were able to discriminate in their hiring, but not in their tax-funded social services programs. As a result of Bush's rule, our government now funds agencies that hire only "Christians," leaving people of other faiths and even Christians who don't agree with their agenda with a dwindling number of social services jobs. The Florida Department of Corrections, a government agency, appears to be following the same path.

The Salvation Army has since sought to "Christianize" their social service programs. In New York City, supervisors were required to provide a list of gay employees and have their staff report on their church attendance. A Jewish supervisor was terminated after she refused to meet these demands. Homeless people I see in my practice tell me they are hounded by proselytizers when they seek services at the Salvation Army. Some are so disturbed by the hounding that they will not return to the Salvation Army for further assistance.

We now also have faith-based prisons proselytizing to the inmates. *Are they preaching the subjugation of women?* Lawtey Correctional Institution, the first of these, is located a few miles from the State Prison where I worked.

Almost a third of schools with sex education programs are teaching "abstinence only" even though as Goldman points out, the states where this is most prominent have the highest divorce and teen pregnancy rates. While abstinence programs seem to delay sex in teens, in the end, they produce higher pregnancy rates.

Homeschoolers are being educated with their own parallel world text books which teach creationism, which has itself created a 6,000 year chronology of the Bible. They are also teaching distorted paranoid notions of Christian persecution by a humanist society. The push is on to bring these distorted texts into public schools as well, and has succeeded in some places. They now frequently substitute the less known term "intelligent design" for creationism.

In seeking greater wealth (often in the name of Jesus) good paying manufacturing jobs have been sent overseas, leaving masses of the population to work in low paying service jobs. While only *8 percent* of American purchases in 1960 were foreign goods, today nearly *60 percent* of our purchases are manufactured overseas. Only about *12 percent* of US jobs are now manufacturing jobs. We also apparently owe the deregulation under President Reagan that added to our current economic woes to the fundamentalist movement.

Chris Hedges points out that our liberal notions of tolerance have gone too far. We have been tolerating the intolerable. While our democratic society is based on tolerance, we can no longer tolerate those who destroy that tolerance. Our passivity is threatening not only our way of life, but perhaps our lives themselves as these zealots seek to destroy all those who oppose them.

The Problem: Fundamentalist Morality

Fundamentalist beliefs involve a simplistic, black and white way of thinking, which compartmentalizes good and bad as if they had no overlap, and views any suggestion that there might be grey as a threat. Fundamentalists look at the church as the absolute source of knowledge of what is moral. All feeling is removed from moral decision-making - one must follow the church's law in every situation. Intuition is denied; people are taught not to listen to their own internal voice. They are told if they find themselves questioning anything the church says, that it is the devil who is trying to veer them off the righteous road. Hence, the inner voice is distorted into the enemy.

It's not only feeling and intuition which are turned off by fundamentalism, but also independent thinking. In his 1940's book, *You Are the Adventure,* J. Allen Boone laments that the average person surrenders "independent thinking" to "mass thinking," creating an "organized ignorance" which keeps him submissive.

This fundamentalist way of thinking can translate into a belief that there is only one right way of doing things just as there is only one path to heaven. In the extreme, it results in obsessive-compulsive behavior and a feeling that life is out of control if everything is not perfectly in place or a daily schedule cannot be followed exactly. Because fundamentalism teaches that the devil is responsible for the bad in the world and God for the good, they do not have a sense that they are responsible for the lives they create or that they have any control over their world. The unknown is seen as dangerous rather than exciting when there is no feeling of control over one's life. There is an aversion to learning or doing new things, and a resistance to change.

All knowledge comes from authorities, devaluing one's own capacity to learn anything. Learning becomes a passive process of being taught – not exploring and learning on one's own. Our school system is set up on this same premise. Children passively sit while the teaching authorities pass out the knowledge. This teaches children that knowledge is something that comes from others, not from their own experience. They learn to defer to the experts even when their own experience contradicts what the experts are telling them. This carries on into adulthood, when they defer to their church's authority and vote for politicians who do not serve their interests.

Fundamentalism does not consider the fact that we can only know the world from our own subjective viewpoint. Philosophers for centuries have pondered whether we even see the same colors. Societal beliefs have been notoriously mistaken. For centuries the world was believed to be flat. Linear theories of causality have now been replaced by Quantum theories. There is little about which we can be certain. Knowing truth objectively is impossible.

Because we cannot know the world objectively, our judgments are often wrong and our interpretations of events change over time. We may initially think of losing a job or a relationship as a terrible punishment by the Universe/God or just bad luck until we find ourselves in a better job or relationship. It then seems that losing the old job or relationship was really good fortune – a blessing in disguise. Likewise, with greater experience, our understanding of what is moral evolves over time. Hence, our moral judgments are commensurate with the level of evolution of our consciousness. We evolve through experiencing being wrong in our judgments time after time, and becoming conscious of our fallibility and the fallibility of others in our lives. This includes those who teach us religious ethics and their interpretation of the Bible, which could just as easily be interpreted in an opposite fashion.

To know the universe objectively, we would have to know the realm of the unknown. Perhaps we need to know God's plan for us or what we chose to learn before we came into the world for our lives to make sense. Because our knowledge is subjective and our moral knowledge is commensurate with our life experiences, education, and consequent level of consciousness, our truth is relative and changes over time.

Fundamentalist claims of objective truth go against everything history has taught us and everything science has discovered. These claims only generate conflict and serve to separate people. Recognizing the relativity of knowledge, including moral knowledge, opens us up to other's viewpoints. Hope for peace in our world depends upon this recognition.

Fundamentalists are taught to accept church interpretation on faith. It must be accepted on faith because there's a low degree of interconnectedness among their belief systems and a great deal of contradiction. So while they reject the notion of the relativity of morality, they are able to condemn abortion as murder and yet glorify murder during war. They can claim the moral superiority of men even though the number of men in prison for all types of crimes greatly exceeds the number of women. Nothing has to make sense in terms of the real world. Our ability to think and to feel become dangerous to this movement.

I have a friend of many years, who has always been a devout Christian. I knew her relationship with her husband had been strained for some time, but was still surprised to hear that she was filing for divorce. She said that she had prayed and prayed until she finally knew in her heart and soul what she needed to do, and that she was now at peace with it. She was upset, though, that when she told a pastor friend of her praying and reaching the difficult decision to divorce her husband, he told her that God didn't want her to get a divorce and that she should come to him for some counseling. She boldly asked him if he didn't hear what she had just said. She had already spent many hours talking the whole thing over with God, and she knew with certainty now what she needed to do. He quoted scripture to her, and she quoted back. "The Bible says, 'If your eye offends you, cut it out.' Well pastor, my husband offends me and I'm cutting him out." She further told him that her relationship was directly with God and that God would not appreciate him trying to interfere with that relationship.

Unfortunately, this is what many churches have the arrogance to do – elevate themselves above God. My friend was strong enough in her own truth that she wasn't about to let the church come between her and God. Fundamentalist churches try to stifle that relationship.

There tends to be a natural hierarchy of values with preservation of life probably at the top. The good people who hid Anne Frank and her family from the Nazi's probably did not feel a lot of remorse at having to lie to authorities about who all lived in their house. While they may have valued the truth and felt it unethical to tell a falsehood in many situations, the value of saving lives so eclipsed the belief that they should tell the truth that this did not likely create a lot of conflict for them. An inner sense of what was right and humane likely guided their decision.

Fundamentalism creates the false belief that only the church-defined moral conscience counts. Fundamentalists may not have attempted to save Anne Frank and her family as they believe anyone who was not "saved" in the right church was lost anyway and deserved any punishment that came their way. Without the feeling component, without empathy, fundamentalists can punish even those they are close to. Rigid beliefs and a total externalization of the moral code result in immoral rather than moral decisions.

Our immoral prison system exists by virtue of the exclusion of feelings and inner guidance from the judicial system. Good judges are frustrated by their inability to use their own inner judgment in a black and white system.

In prisons corrections officers are taught that the ultimate moral law is "security sticks together." As in totalitarian fundamentalism, loyalty to the system is paramount. The worst sin a corrections officer can commit is to report another officer. Whatever atrocities are committed will not be reported as it is the reporter of the crime who will be punished by the system – not the perpetrator. As I have witnessed, the feelings suppressed by the corrections system later come out as nightmares, flashbacks, and intrusive thoughts of the abuse committed.

We are born with a good connection to our own inner moral compass, our intuition and feeling. Children are by nature curious and creative, but authoritarian parenting, chaotic lifestyles resulting from drug and alcohol abuse, fundamentalist religion, and a school system based on memorizing rather than thinking and creating separates us from our inner compass.

I've known children, who were very creative in their early years and had absolutely no sense of urgency about anything. They would turn a box into a space ship, loved to dress up in costumes, and could stay in the world of make-believe all day long. Going through school and religious training, their natural openness to experience was distorted to the point that they have now become quite concrete and extremely compulsive. They plan everything in detail and become very upset if they have to change their plan. They don't like to rethink any decision.

While liberal Christianity has espoused the "Golden Rule," teaching that we should treat others (regardless of their religious beliefs or other differences) as we want to be treated ourselves, fundamentalism's emphasis is on punishing people who deviate from the church's doctrine. Inclusivity and tolerance are distorted into exclusivity and punishment of deviators. Love turns to hate. It's them against the rest of the world, and no outsider is safe. They have declared war on all of us who disagree with them.

For centuries, religions have persecuted and tried to control women due to their greater intuition and feeling functions. The socialization of boys in our culture early on helps suppress this part of their being. But more essential than that, as Dr. Amen's brain scan studies show, men's brains (at least in Western cultures) do not appear to be wired the same way so that their capacity for empathy is not typically as great as that of women. When confronted by the inner conscience of their wives, powerful men are inhibited in oppressing people. It's harder for women to disconnect from their inner voices and this presents a great threat to those who attempt to deceive and control us. Fundamentalism tries to silence women altogether. So they declare that we are inferior and that what we say has no value.

Religion has been traditionally used by the wealthy to control the poor. Studies have shown that it's the poor and undereducated of below average intelligence who are most easily deceived by the distorted beliefs of the fundamentalists. However, a lifetime of brainwashing can ensnare even otherwise bright people.

The Origins of My Uncertainty

You might be wondering how I acquired my inside knowledge of fundamentalist behavior when I have never been a fundamentalist myself. The answer to that is: I have lived among them. In fact, I unknowingly lived among them long before I moved to North Florida. It just took me a very long time to realize that what was going on in my life had a deeper, darker motive than I could ever have imagined.

There were early signs that something was wrong, but I didn't have the conceptual framework to put things together. I knew I came from fundamentalist stock. My grandmother had told me that she wasn't allowed to play cards as a child. She liked to explain the moral significance of every movie she took me to on Friday nights at the Linda Theatre back when we all lived on Goodyear Blvd in Akron. Then once when I was visiting her on a college break, we watched Neil Armstrong's walk on the moon together, and she told me that what was happening on television was all government fraud – everyone knows that heaven is up where the stars are and no one can go there without dying. The moon walk was filmed somewhere in Arizona. My grandmother was my first recognized exposure to the irrationality of fundamentalism. I just thought it was hilarious.

My parents had outgrown their fundamentalist roots, considered themselves much more modern than my grandmother, liked to play bridge, and definitely believed in science. However, politically, they were Goldwater Republicans. My father impressed upon me early on that communists were trying to ruin the country and take over the world. Countries would fall like dominoes if we didn't contain the communist threat. Management was good; unions were bad. Life was simple black and white. I never understood the whys.

My upbringing wasn't exactly the typical American experience of the time, which probably helped me learn to think.

111

When I was eight years old and my father was promoted into management at Goodyear International, they took my young, impressionable mind to Argentina – a new culture, new religion, new ideological perspectives. The clashing of the cultures spurned a questioning of most everything I was told. There were so many contradictions in what I was being taught and witnessing. Where in all this was truth? I couldn't avoid imbibing the flavor of this Catholic country, the Latin emotionality, and the worldliness of the big city. This new world opened up my parents too to some extent. My engineer father told me that reincarnation made more sense than just living once and dying – energy doesn't disappear – it only changes form. There's so much to learn that it only makes sense that we should evolve over many lifetimes.

My mother was the first mom in the neighborhood to get on "the pill." The 60's brought a new openness to ideas around the entire globe. There was a new awakening – a new freedom of thought. The Methodist church we went to embraced the freedom of the times. In Sunday school I was taught of a loving, forgiving God that wants children to be happy. Jesus loves all the children – "red and yellow, black and white, they are precious in his sight."

However, Americans were not welcomed by all in Argentina. We arrived just after Castro had taken Cuba and Che Guevara was hiding out in Northern Argentina. The graffiti on building walls declaring, "YANKEE GO HOME" gave the message clearly enough, although on one overpass on the way to the airport someone with a sense of humor added – "BY PANAM," and made us laugh every time we went by. The anti-American sentiment was felt more strongly when the Goodyear factory was set on fire and we had bomb threats made to our home. There were two plain clothed cops on our corner for some time and we were told not to speak English on buses or trains. Weren't we supposed to be the good guys? I learned to suspend judgment at an early age.

The Argentine government was very unstable after Juan Peron and there were revolutions just about every year with the chiefs of branches of the armed services fighting each other for control. Having watched a lot of old World War II movies where the Army and Navy guys got into barroom brawls, in my child's mind, I thought for a long time that armies everywhere fought navies. That was my childhood understanding of the nature of war.

We lived near an Army camp and it was hard to tell when they were practicing maneuvers or when there was actually a revolution going on. My older brother showed me how to use this to our advantage to get out of school. We'd tell the principal that there was a lot of bombing going on at the army camp and that our mother wanted us to come home early. When we got home from school, we'd tell our mother that the principal thought we should come home early as there was rumor of another revolution. We lived an hour from school and they never seemed to compare notes because we never got caught.

True revolution days were like hurricane days in Florida. They may be scary, but they got us out of school so there was some celebrating going on. My parents told us we were safe; they had an escape plan. Sometimes my mother would pack the suitcases. I was hopeful for an adventure (and a prolonged time away from school), but we never had to flee.

Somehow the freedom of the "Make Love Not War" era didn't extend to my parents' politics. I think that being the target of the anger of the Argentine populace had a very different effect on them than it did on me. They didn't seem to question who the good guys actually were as I did. They just seemed to buckle down even deeper into their belief in the righteousness and infallibility of the great United States of America.

The poverty in Argentina tugged at my child's heart. I volunteered at an orphanage with my church youth group, sleeping on damp, cold beds in the winter with the orphans. They had no heaters and we slept in our jeans and coats. Even so I shivered all night. Most children were not at the orphanage because their parents died, but because their parents could not afford to care for them.

At home, raggedly clad children came begging at our gate and I let them in to play basketball with us and jump on the trampoline much to my mother's chagrin. My mother brought out day old bread for them. I insisted they get something good to eat. I snuck out the best of our junk food – homemade cake and cookies. My mother usually relented and made them a bologna sandwich with fresh bread. The contrast of the lot of these children with our own privileged lifestyle seemed so unfair. We may have been middle class folks in the US, but in Argentina we lived the good life replete with servants and country club, where I spent much of my childhood riding my horse, swimming, and playing tennis with the other privileged people. I watched Prince Phillip play polo at our club and my parents had dinner with Queen Elizabeth.

A pacifist was invited to speak at our school (could this even happen now?). He was a Vietnam vet speaking against the war. He told the boys that they had options; people were fleeing to Canada. He believed that the commandment, "Thou shalt not kill," should not be suspended in the case of war. When I took this back to my father, he was not pleased. He was a Seabee in the Pacific during World War II. Warriors were heroes – everyone knows that. Even so, my father had always refused to tell me much about his war experiences, except that there was an intellectually challenged guy in his unit that he took care of. I knew war was a sensitive subject for my father. Feeling his pain, I declared that the world would be a better place if there were more pacifists and people didn't have to fight wars. I was going to be a pacifist.

Years later, when the Berlin wall fell, my father's mantra changed from "the communists are trying to ruin the country" to "the liberals are trying to ruin the country." My brothers joined the chant, but I strayed from the holy grail of Republicanism. I was the rebel – the liberal daughter who did not buy the corporate party line. They sent me off to a conservative Baptist college, probably hoping that my liberalism was just a stage. While bored out of my skull studying for a history test at the library my first year in college, I wrote:

> The Silence disturbs the Thinkers,
> Whose every thoughts are like wheels
> Turning in a clock,
> Precipitated by others who merely wind them
> And watch them run.

I still remember this mostly, I think, because of my friends' reaction to what I wrote. This was an era where art and creativity

114

were valued. I was not mocked for expressing myself, but they politely told me they did not get it. One friend suggested that precipitation had to do with rain and that it couldn't be used as a verb. I guess even then I was aware that most people do not think independently, aren't aware that they don't, and that most of our studies did not encourage thinking. There were, however, some wonderfully freeing ideas flowing from some classes even at this conservative college. I was particularly taken with Jean-Paul Sartre and the whole existential school of thought.

I don't really know when the shift came. Fundamentalist religion somehow became more unyieldingly attached to Republican ideology, and I guess to stay loyal to the Republican, corporate cause, my parents shifted with the wind, coming full circle back to their irrational religious roots in their elder years. I was actually unaware that this shift had taken place until years later. They didn't speak to me about their beliefs. They just acted on them. It was a secret to be kept from me. Such was their training, I guess.

Even so, my parents' buying back into fundamentalism was pretty inconsistent and probably motivated by fear. My mother started refusing to go to church. She became increasingly paranoid and psychiatric treatment did little to help her. Even after her death, my father would not go to church except when I took him on Christmas Eve. My father still read every natural medicine book I gave him, and took any supplement I thought might help him. However, he seemed afraid to let people know that I was taking him for unorthodox Frequency Specific Microcurrent treatments for his prostate cancer. When his urologist asked him how he had reduced his PSA so drastically, he said that he didn't know. Perhaps he didn't want to be seen as disloyal to the party, which supports only traditional medicine. To his credit, unlike some other Republican, fundamentalist relatives, who ripped out my heart with their rejection and punishing behavior, he never could bring himself to turn against his wayward daughter and was regrettably probably punished for his failure to isolate me. While I was frustrated by his superficial adherence to nonsense, he undoubtedly knew more about the dangers of doing otherwise than he disclosed. He repeatedly warned me not to confront the people who harassed me.

So it was not only my experiences working with fundamentalists in prison and living among them in North Florida that educated me about their ways. That I was able to look for my own answers to the eternal questions that all religions attempt to answer and tolerate the ambiguity of not knowing can probably be attributed to my somewhat unconventional upbringing in a particular era in time. It wasn't that my parents didn't try to indoctrinate me in their beliefs. I was just exposed to too many other realities for it to take.

When the power of love
overcomes the love of power,
the world will know peace.

Jimi Hendrix

Our prime purpose in this life is to help others. And if
you can't help them, at least don't hurt them.

Dalai Lama

Human Rights are not only violated by terrorism,
repression or assassination, but also by unfair economic
structures that create huge inequalities.

Pope Francis

An eye for an eye only ends up making the whole world
blind.

Mahatma Ghandi

Chapter VII

A Solution

Achieving Peace:

If we are to have peace in the world, people must be able to see beyond the "one right way" of fundamentalism, develop the potential to see multiple perspectives, and tolerate the ambiguity of not knowing what God's will is. We need to acknowledge that fundamentalism is a primitive level of cognitive and moral development which is dangerous to our society. It is divisive and intolerant of dissent. We can no longer pretend that it is OK to be concrete and think in black and white. It's not OK! It's causing war after war after war while each group tries to prove that their group's "one right way" is better than the other group's "one right way."

Studies show that both life experiences and higher education may be able to reverse the distortion in thinking which is brought on by authoritarian parenting, our educational system, and fundamentalist indoctrination. Undoubtedly, this is why fundamentalists are so opposed to higher education. True education teaches people to think and listen to their own inner guidance. Unfortunately, this is not currently taught in our public schools and even is lacking in some of our colleges.

Rather than encouraging our children to memorize facts to meet the requirements of the state exam, it is much more important that we teach children to think, listen to their inner voices, and to own their own feelings. Lessons in psychology, sociology, logic, philosophy and anthropology as well as international travel broaden our ability to view the world with perspective. Learning a second language shows there is more than one way of saying the same thing, and may broaden perspective as well. Art, music, and drama feed creativity.

Experimental schools, which make learning experiences available to children and allow them to choose what and when they want to learn, give children the opportunity to direct their own learning experiences and develop a sense that they can gain knowledge on their own – not just from external authorities. These experimental schools have shown that children learn what they need to know when they see a reason to do so.

Cognitive psychology helps us see the world from multiple perspectives, allowing us to reframe our life traumas in a way that they do not cause us such pain. As a psychologist I know that I have to move people out of their limited black and white, catastrophizing view of their situation to a place where they can see things from another perspective to help them move out of their pain. Cognitive psychology can help people develop an ability to see multiple perspectives, increasing the potential for a more advanced level of relativistic thinking. Including psychology classes in our schools can help children achieve a higher level of cognitive and moral growth at an earlier age. Many other countries around the world already include psychology classes in their schools while in this country, where we have so much violence, psychology is not included in the curriculum.

I once saw a veteran who had committed an insane act during an insane war. He had been beating himself up for twenty years for doing something he thought was unforgivable, and had become so anxious that he rarely left home and could not work. He burst into tears as he told me that he knew he was going to hell. I asked him if he would condemn his own son to eternal damnation if he had done the same. He replied that he certainly would not. He loved his son and would want him to learn from his mistakes and go on to live a happy life. I asked him why he thought that a God he called his father would be so insane and punishing as to not forgive him and want the best for him as he did his own son. Would he not expect that God must be at least as good and forgiving as he was? He had never thought of it that way. A new perspective lifted a heavy weight he'd been carrying for years. Too many churches teach of an insane, punishing God that is totally inconsistent with any concept that "God is Good." This causes immense pain to many who fear the eternal punishment of this idea of God which has nothing to do with what the Bible teaches.

In his book, *The Biology of Belief*, Dr. Bruce Lipton, a cell biologist, points out that the most widespread and insidious form of human violence is *ideological control*. Religious movements and governments throughout history have repeatedly prodded their constituents into aggression and violence to deal with dissenters and nonbelievers. He says that *"Survival of the Most Loving"* is the only ethic that will ensure both a healthy personal life and a healthy planet. He also points out that in the world of cell biology as in the outer world it is not survival of the fittest, but survival of the most cooperative that is the rule. We need to put kindness and cooperation above competition in our schools, our work places, and our lives.

Prison Reform:

The prison system is an ineffective, obsolete system, whose purpose has become self-preservation. In an attempt to continue its existence, laws have been created that endanger our society. People can be arrested and brought back to prison for very trivial violations. With this kind of threat to large parts of the population, law enforcement increases their control of the community outside of prison as well. The idea of sending people to prison to protect the public seems to have gotten lost somewhere. Now people are being sent to prison to preserve the jobs of the prison workers and the income of the prison contractors. It was almost an everyday occurrence at the reception center, to see employees laugh when citizens came back to prison on these ridiculous "violation of probation" convictions, declaring that these laws were their "job security." Is this really the kind of society we want to be? Why have we accepted this so long? These laws need to be changed now!

Prisons in this country were originally intended to protect the public from dangerous people. People came to this country to escape debtor's prisons, and yet we have now created the same sort of system, which we keep because the system has created "job security" for people in areas where there is no other industry and kept rich contractors in business. To put people in prison for failing to pay traffic tickets or for nonpayment of child support makes no sense at all. Are we getting the fines or child support paid by keeping these people locked up? Of course not! What we're doing is putting more children on AFDC for the rest of us to support, while disrupting the lives of countless families, and making it even more difficult for the offenders to find jobs when they get out of prison as they will then have a criminal record.

If the oppressiveness of nations were judged by the number of people in their prisons, the United States would win the prize as the most oppressive nation in the world with a whopping 25% of the whole world's prisoners in our prisons. When there are almost 200 countries in the world, it's embarrassing that we lead the world with a quarter of the world's prisoners.

When I wrote Florida Governor Scott of the problems with the prison system, I offered to volunteer two days a week to help reform the system. He did not take me up on my offer. I'm proposing these new guidelines for our prison system anyway:

1. The consequences should be related to the offense. This has been a vital principle in parenting classes for years. If a child colors on the wall, you don't take away her birthday party, you make her clean the wall. If you owe money, you should have to work and pay it back. That's what we call a logical consequence. We have already set up a system to take child support payments out of people's wages. Could we not just garnish the wages or take the tax returns of people who fail to pay traffic tickets or other fines as well? How about giving them community service hours? If people are not working, they obviously can't pay their child support. So why do we put them in prison as if this will solve the problem?

When I was doing my residency (for little pay), I also taught court-ordered classes for domestic violence and sex offenders. Domestic violence offenders could be siblings fighting over the TV remote or someone who threw ice at her boyfriend. There were people given the sex offender label who had pee'd by the roadside or were caught having sex at the beach.

I also substitute taught for a number of other classes, including one called, "Felony Values." During one of these felony classes, I asked the offenders (most of which had been convicted of theft) if they would continue to steal if they had to work until they paid back the person the value of what they had stolen from them. They all laughed and said they much preferred prison to having to work and having their money taken from them. In other words, they saw losing their own money as a major deterrent. It wouldn't be worth stealing if you had to pay the money back. You see, the one thing that the antisocial personality values most is *money*. Would it not be more logical (and cost-effective) to sentence these people to work programs to pay back people (or their insurance companies) the amount they stole? Maybe even with interest? What happened to sentencing offenders of this type to the military (or a civilian work corps), where their wages could be easily garnished? Maybe our insurance rates would even go down.

Taking that idea of the consequence fitting the crime, why shouldn't violent offenders have to work in prison and support their victims or the families of the victims that were affected by their crimes? If they kill someone, the consequence should be that they have to pay support to their victim's children, spouse, or aging parents for the rest of their lives. If they maim someone, they should have to pay their hospital bills and support them until they can work or provide them with the same amount of disability payments as they would get from social security. This would be a logical consequence, and actually serve as a deterrent. How is locking people up with nothing to do all day accomplishing anything?

2. Exchange the goal of *punishment* for one of creating independent, responsible citizens. While punishment is not a stated goal of the Florida Department of Corrections, corrections officers have taken upon themselves what they consider to be the main purpose of their jobs - the punishment of criminals. Consequently, prisoners are frequently beaten and harassed by security. *Let's take religion out of our corrections system.* Rather than emphasizing *punishing* people (especially for things they often cannot avoid), would it not be more reasonable to emphasize problem-solving and goal-directed activity to accomplish what we as a society want to achieve? The purpose of prisons is to protect society. Let's keep it at that.

3. Prison programs should be self-supporting. Why should we, the law-abiding citizens of this country, be burdened by having to support people in prison? Prisons used to grow their own produce and raise their own livestock. While the Florida

Department of Corrections states that Florida prisoners are growing some produce, they are far from being self-sufficient. Whatever happened to the idea that prisoners should have to support themselves like the rest of us? Let's get rid of the catering companies that our wealthy presidents brought in to make themselves even richer.

4. Stop privatizing prisons and jails. Privatizing prisons is handing the care of inmates to those who seek to profit from them. I met a number of prisoners who had been in privatized county jails, where they were denied the medication they needed to increase the profit of the corporation. I saw one inmate who was denied the insulin he needed to control his diabetes and almost died while in jail. I saw several inmates with Bipolar Disorder who were told they did not need their medication – they were given relaxation training to treat their chemical imbalance. We can only expect more negligence when jails and prisons are run by profiteers.

5. Quit taking away people's driver's licenses. The State not so cleverly takes away people's driver's licenses when they cannot pay their child support or traffic tickets, ensuring in many areas without public transportation, that they will be unable to work, and thus end up in jail or prison because they still cannot pay their child support or fines. Would we not better accomplish our goals by setting up work programs for people who cannot pay their child support? We could employ those corrections officers no longer needed in prisons to administer these programs, which could be very similar to work release programs, except that the offenders could go home in the evenings and other working citizens would not have to pay for their room and board. Of course these corrections officers would be monitored so they don't decide to *punish* the workers.

6. Sentence substance abusers to substance abuse treatment programs instead of to prison. Studies have shown that substance abuse treatment programs cost half of what prisons cost us, yet we continue to put substance abusers in prison with very little substance abuse treatment available to them. Work programs for substance abusers should, of course, also be self-supporting.

It is appropriate for substance abusers who actually pose a danger driving, to lose their licenses until they obtain treatment and are clean and sober for a year. They should be sentenced to substance abuse/work programs with housing so they do not need to drive to work. If they are able to stay clean and sober for a year, they should get their licenses back. A year could be added on for the second offense. On the third offense, they could be sentenced to a work program with no chance of getting back their license until they are clean and sober for ten years.

7. Only imprison people to protect the public. This is the stated mission of the Florida Department of Corrections – to protect the public. We need to decriminalize or reduce sentences to fines on crimes that do not cause injury to the public. We could really reduce our costs by legalizing marijuana and it looks like steps are finally being taken to do that in the State of Florida. In fact, the State would raise abundant revenue by levying taxes on the sale of marijuana, and put some drug dealers out of business at the same time. We need a national decriminalization of marijuana next. We're all aware of the deleterious effects of excessive alcohol and marijuana, and there should be consequences for driving under the influence of either, but who really thinks people who smoke marijuana are otherwise dangerous and need to be monitored in some way?

8. Protect the public from the truly dangerous people. We're not currently doing so well with this one. I have firsthand knowledge of the very dangerous people who will be released back onto the public. They are in confinement either due to the violent nature of their crimes or because they were too violent to be allowed to stay in the general population of inmates after coming to prison. In either case, if they were to learn to behave while in confinement, (unless they were on death row), they would eventually be allowed to work their way up the levels to the general population of inmates. However, many of these inmates do not manage to learn to interact with people well enough to get out of confinement, and yet are released back into society when their terms are up. Does this make sense? If we did not lock up people who do not pay their debts, we could afford to sentence the truly dangerous people to life terms and keep them there for life.

9. Provide alternative facilities for people with mental health issues. Another problem with our corrections system is the large number of people who actually belong in long-term, mental health

treatment rather than in prisons. When I worked at the reception center where North Florida inmates were screened, a good percentage of the inmates required mental health treatment. There are "psych camps" set up for these inmates rather than mental health treatment facilities. Many inmates deny their mental health issues on intake and go untreated during their stay in prison, because of the violent reputation of the "psych camps." Of course, if we had universal health insurance and these people could receive their medication on a regular basis, then many would not be in prison or need psychiatric hospitalization anyway. As it is, if all goes well, upon their release from prison, they will be given an appointment at a mental health center (which most likely they won't be able to afford) and an appointment for a social security disability evaluation. If they qualify for disability, they will be awarded Medicaid and will be able to get their psych meds. If not, they will likely continue to prey upon society until they are once again incarcerated. In keeping with the goal of minimizing the expense to other working citizens, these persons with mental health issues should have to work whenever they are able so they can support their programs. Purposeful work is vital to self-esteem and mental health, and any able-bodied person should be working.

10.   Create transitional work programs. Inmates are given a group IQ test at admission, which has shown that large numbers of these inmates function at a borderline level (just above what we used to call mentally retarded) intellectually. In a challenging job market, these people are not going to be able to support themselves. They will need work programs (probably with housing for many) in order to be functioning members of society upon their release. Actually, a transitional work program for all inmates would be beneficial.

11.   Erase the prison records of people who have been incarcerated for unpaid debts. It is our great shame that we have destroyed families by arresting people for unpaid child support and unpaid fines. Let's stop this outrage now!

12.   Provide better monitoring of state prisons by the federal government and better training for the corrections officers, including classes in psychology. Conduct periodic confidential focus groups and individual interviews of prison workers off site to keep track of what's going on.

13.   Let's recognize that the poor in this country do not get an adequate defense from pro bono attorneys and expand paid legal aid staff to defend at least those charged with felonies. Paralegals could do much of the work for attorneys to present the cases in court.

14.   Stop targeting minorities and alternative lifestyles. According to Time magazine, while African-Americans only comprise 13% of the population of the United States, they comprise 37% of the prison population. When I taught classes for sex offenders, the great majority of the class was composed of gay men – men who were caught having sex on the beach or peeing in a park. Where were the heterosexuals who had sex on the beach or pee'd behind a tree? Apparently, they did not get arrested for what is a crime for gay men.

15.   Restore at a national level the voting rights of persons with felonies at the end of their sentence. This one is related to targeting minorities. If more minorities go to prison, then more minorities will be unable to vote. Last year, Florida voters decided to restore the rights of the imprisoned after their release, but many other states have not.

To summarize, the corrections system does not work, yet we have continued to do more of the same. We build more prisons and get more repeat offenders. I think it's time we try something different that might have a chance of creating a better, kinder society.

Prevention:

Let's look further into the effects of natural supplements on mental disorders. If as studies have shown, lack of lithium in the soil and water correlates with significant increases in five major crime rates, perhaps we need to make supplements available to the entire population in areas where the soil and water are deficient.

A lot of anxiety, compulsive behaviors, and psychosis are related to the decrease in oxygen in our atmosphere. Much of anxiety and even hallucinations are mediated by bacteria in our brains. Sufficient levels of oxygen in the body eat up those bacteria reducing anxiety and eliminating hallucinations.

Supplementation with Co-Q10/Ubiquinol raises oxygen levels in the body sufficiently to do this.

More studies are needed to explore the benefits of supplementation. We also need to look more closely at the effects of GMO crops on our mental health.

*I think our government ought to stay out of
the prayer business.*

Jimmy Carter

*I believe in an America where the separation of church
and state is absolute – where no Catholic prelate would tell
the President (should he be Catholic) how to act, and
no Protestant minister would tell his parishioners for
whom to vote – where no church or church school is granted
any public funds or political preference – and where
no man is denied public office merely because his religion
differs from the president who might appoint him or
the people who might elect him.*

John F. Kennedy

*...the morality of the priesthood and the devotion of
the people have been manifestly increased by the total
separation of the Church and the State.*

James Madison

*Believing with you that religion is a matter which lies
solely between man and his God...
I contemplate with sovereign reverence that act of the
whole American people which declared that their legislature
should "make no law respecting an establishment of religion, or
prohibiting the free exercise thereof;" thus building a
wall of separation between Church and State.*

Thomas Jefferson

*Politics is the most important of the civil activities and has its
own field of action, which is not that of religion.*

Pope Francis

Chapter VIII

Other Government Programs:

Creating Democracy in America

Our prison system is only one small reflection of our failing democracy. Having worked with a number of other government programs over the years, I would say that the rest of our government needs updating as well. Since we've entered a new millennium, we should be able to make some modifications to the constitution so our courts don't have to work so hard to try to interpret it to fit current issues.

Creating a Democracy:

Let's not delude ourselves by equating democracy and capitalism. As Michael Moore aptly pointed out, they are not one and the same. Democracy is rule by the people. Capitalism has proven to be rule by the wealthy. Somehow we have been brainwashed to believe they are the same, and defend those greedy profiteers who keep us down. How many of us voted to have high interest rates? How many of us voted to lose our homes if we cannot pay our taxes or miss a few payments on our mortgages even if we have been paying that mortgage for years and have more than paid the purchase price? These decisions are not made by the people – they're made by our wealthy rulers. Things have really not changed since the feudal days when the wealthy lords could steal the land from the peasants when they could not pay their taxes. We believe in something called the American Dream, and have been brought up to believe the American Dream is only possible in a capitalist system, when this system is actually what keeps us from having our share of the pie.

I was taught that education would bring me an easier life – maybe even some wealth. And maybe in the past this was true, but under the great equalizer of capitalism, everyone but the very wealthy rulers will struggle. My grandfather, who had a high school education and worked in a factory, had a higher standard of living than I have, and was able to retire. I have a Ph.D. - the highest level of education in my field - and yet I only get by month to month on my income, live in a small house, and cannot possibly live in retirement at close to the standard I did while working. I have paid the maximum amount of taxes as a small business owner (about 30% of my income went to taxes and social security/Medicare), yet my social security alone will not provide me with enough money to retire comfortably because my government chose to spend my money elsewhere. *Did we vote to let the government spend our social security elsewhere?* Invested properly, we would have had ample money to retire. If we're all struggling to survive, we don't have time to question what our rulers tell us. If we could all afford to retire, we'd have time to get involved and monitor our government more closely. We don't have time to think. We march off to war like robots, not questioning that the great United States would ever be in the wrong. Those who dare to question government policies are labeled "un-American." Yet our duty as American citizens is to question. The true patriots are those who question our government's policies and try to keep them honest. We can only be led around like fools if we follow fools without questioning their policies.

Democracy means the people make the decisions. That new golden rule that says that *"those with the most gold make the rules"* needs to be put in check. In order to be a true democracy, we need to restructure our government. If we got rid of the Electoral College (who can explain why we need this?) and voted directly for the candidates, we could save a ton of money and reduce the influence of the wealthy. We wouldn't feel like we were robbed when the electoral votes did not reflect the popular vote. What's the point of having a popular vote when we have an electoral college that can overturn our vote?

If we are to take back our government from private interests, we need to be voting on the big issues ourselves. Our representatives should be asking us how we want them to vote. We are now in the computer age; we could vote from home. We could print out our vote, sign it, and mail it in or drop it off at a voting drop box so the results could be confirmed manually. If the representative does not vote as the majority vote indicates, we should be able to impeach the representative. I'm frequently being asked to write my legislators about my opinions on a variety of bills, which I do on a regular basis. How much harder would it be for those legislators to ask our opinions on the bills up for consideration?

I believe the American people would do a better job of decision-making than the rich people in congress. I don't know anyone who would have voted to spend billions of dollars rebuilding a levy system for a city below sea level, especially in an age of global warming. We could have moved the city of New Orleans up river and built a sort of Jazz Branson for all that money.

And I think we'd be a little more cautious about sending our children off to war. We'd check our facts and exhaust all other possibilities before sending our young people off to die or get maimed. We certainly wouldn't sacrifice our children so that already rich people could get richer.

Rather than having primarily lawyers, who are by nature and training adversarial, in government, we would be better to employ psychologists and other mental health professionals, who are trained in problem-solving, mediation, and peacekeeping. Does our president have a psychologist among his inner circle? I don't think so. He has experts on war advising him, but no experts on peace. We need a Department of Peace! It's no wonder we engage in so many wars when we only have a war-oriented Defense Department and no Peace Department. We need to downscale and reorient our Defense Department away from American Imperialism to protecting our boundaries (and I don't mean by building a wall).

We the people need to take the power we've been told the people have in a democracy, and make this country for once, what we've been long claiming to be - a democracy. We need to go beyond the labels, "liberal" and "conservative" to a new paradigm of practical, humane democracy.

Nonprofit organizations typically create mission statements and make goals for the organization. We need to define our mission as a country and make our laws consistent with that mission. Having full-employment as a goal would be nice. How about creating peaceful relations with the rest of the world? That's a novel idea!

Separation of Church and State:

More safeguards need to be put in place to insure the separation of church and state. These pseudo-Christian religious fanatics want to force their religion on everyone else. They have declared war on our way of life and we need to respond to that threat!

We have no infrastructure to handle the many violations of church and state and the harassment of citizens due to their religious beliefs or lack thereof. These disputes are typically handled in the courts, where it can take years to resolve anything. We need a separate federal government agency to monitor issues related to separation of church and state, and infractions of the law by religious groups who think it's their duty to *punish* people into submission to God and men. This insidious movement has gone far enough in removing the barriers between church and state. We need a government organization with the power to bring even Supreme Court decisions to the public vote. Otherwise we subject ourselves to the rule of a group which can easily be taken over by fundamentalists and exert this minority's rule over the rest of us.

We need this agency to monitor our schools and ensure that children are not being brainwashed in fundamentalism. We need to repeal the Supreme Court decision to allow church groups such as the Good News Clubs to meet in schools. We need to get rid of vouchers that are draining funds for our public schools to provide funding for religious schools.

When I was at the prison reception center, the hospital administrator opened staff meetings with a prayer. Government agencies, including the military, need to be monitored so they do not proselytize and punish those who do not conform to their religious beliefs. Prayer groups belong in churches – not in government agencies, schools, or businesses. As I observed while working in the prison system, these groups may be involved in a lot more than just prayer, targeting for harassment individuals who do not conform.

According to the Americans United bulletin, *Church and State,* Air Force Academy cadets in 2006 accused their school teachers of pressuring non-Christians to convert to evangelical Christianity, and until August 2011, the Air Force offered a course called "Christian Just War Theory."

True Christian churches that still believe in a loving, forgiving, inclusive God need to take a lead in countering the attack on all that is good in our society by these pseudo-Christians. One by one we may be able to help the victims of these cults see that they have been conned by those who wish to control them. It's not just the women they want to control. The men are just as subservient to the insanity of these pseudo-Christian cults. Allowing men to control the women in their lives gives them a false sense of control, when they've actually surrendered their own lives to the dictatorship of the church.

Prevention:

Let's look further into the effects of natural supplements on mental disorders. If as studies have shown, lack of lithium in the soil and water correlates with significant increases in five major crime rates, perhaps we need to make supplements available to the entire population in areas where the soil and water are deficient.

A lot of anxiety, compulsive behaviors, and psychosis are related to the decrease in oxygen in our atmosphere. Much of anxiety and even hallucinations are mediated by bacteria in our brains. Sufficient levels of oxygen in the body eat up those bacteria reducing anxiety and eliminating hallucinations. Supplementation with Co-Q10/Ubiquinol raises oxygen levels in the body sufficiently to do this.

More studies are needed to explore the benefits of supplementation. We also need to look more closely at the effects of GMO crops on our mental health.

Monitoring of State Law Enforcement

I can't tell you how many people have told me that I should have *expected* corruption when I moved to a small town. Rather than just accepting corruption in local law enforcement, we need to create a separate agency to monitor state law enforcement agencies, including the local Sheriff's Departments. No one should have to file a complaint with the same agency they're filing the complaint against. Florida voted to create its own Department of Homeland Security in 2018 to deal with local terrorists. It would be good to also have a Federal agency monitoring local Sheriff's Departments.

People who want to decentralize government want to protect the corruption in their states. The only chance we have of enforcing our laws in the states and protecting their citizens is to have monitoring by the Feds.

Women's Rights

It's sad that women still need to defend their right to equal opportunities in this country. Since the Republican religious fanatics are bent on stripping women of our rights, we need our constitution to confirm very clearly and specifically that women are entitled to equal opportunities in education and work, equal pay for equal work, the right to own property, the right to bear arms, the right to hold public office, and of course, the right to vote. Nothing should be taken for granted. Reproductive rights should also be guaranteed constitutionally so the religious right cannot limit us with myths of "legitimate rape" not resulting in pregnancy. We need to let these immoral zealots know that we are not going back to an era where women are the property of men. This country needs to be about freedom for all. Divorced women and never married parents need to be included as a protected group by our government, and crimes against women and nonbelievers in general need to be adjudicated as hate crimes. War has been declared on our way of life and on women in particular, and we must respond to this threat.

Freedom for All

We need to reemphasize that freedom applies to everyone equally in this country. This includes very basic freedoms that we tend to take for granted, including the right to choose how we want to dress and style our hair, what we choose to eat, whom we choose to marry regardless of ethnicity or gender (or to choose not to marry), choose how many children to have or not to have, choose how and where we want to be educated, choose our own careers, and choose where we want to live without being harassed. These rights need to be constitutionally guaranteed so individual states cannot decide to discriminate. The Christian Taliban seeks to limit our freedoms. We need to act now to make sure our freedoms are not further eroded.

Education

We all recognize our current education system is doing a poor job. Children are wasting precious years of their lives in uncomfortable classroom situations, and yet coming out without even basic skills. We've got to quit focusing on memorizing facts to pass a test. Learning should be fun, and our education system takes all the fun out of learning. Historical novels are fun; history texts are not. Learning in the current educational environment is nothing less than torture for many children. We should be encouraging children to explore their own interests and learn to think. Facts can be looked up; there's no need to memorize more than the basics. Children will be excited about learning if we let them follow their interests. The favorite word of three year olds is "why." If left to their own instincts, children will follow their own yearning to learn. Unfortunately, by the time they get through a few years of our boring schools, they've lost all interest in learning.

Children need to be taught to honor their feelings and listen to their own inner voices. Classes in developing intuition could help repair the connection. They need to be taught to question authority and think for themselves so they will grow up with a good moral compass and be good monitors of government.

Because everything else depends upon the basics, it seems useful to spend elementary school focusing on just that, and otherwise allowing children to read whatever interests them, encouraging them to explore their own interests and teach themselves with teachers serving as guides to help them explore. This would take the pressure off children, who tend to develop at different rates and come to hate school in the current system. It would be more productive to have them write and discuss their own opinions on what they have learned. They can learn to think independently, see the world from multiple perspectives, and question authority without worrying about constant tests to see if they have memorized what they have learned.

We've got huge numbers of children being diagnosed with ADHD because the current classroom situation doesn't work for them. Rather than changing the environment to meet the needs of these children, we're medicating them to fit where they don't fit! Often kids with ADHD are very creative and they need an outlet for this creativity. Most classrooms stifle creativity.

Thirty children to one teacher is not efficient. Older children should be paired with younger children and spend a half hour at a time tutoring younger children in basic reading, math, and writing skills. This will reinforce what the older children have already learned while giving the younger children more individualized attention. Children could actually talk to each other about their interests and what they are learning. They would get satisfaction from cooperating and helping others rather than competing with them.

We could actually create a school system where children are treated with respect and enjoy their early years rather than being tortured in schools that punish those who deviate from the norm. Children would have time to play, stay fit, and develop their social skills.

A lawsuit against the State of Michigan was filed for failing to teach children to read. This is not necessarily the fault of the teachers. Many children are not getting the medical evaluations they need to help them read. Children should have full vision and hearing testing by doctors (not untrained volunteers) at school on a yearly basis so they can function optimally in the classroom. They should be tested for perceptual distortions as well as for the clarity of their vision. Schools should be following through to make sure the children get the glasses or hearing aids they need. Children should also be getting their blood sugar levels tested on a yearly basis as this greatly affects their ability to learn.

We need to be teaching the old *Golden Rule* – to treat others the way you want to be treated. We need to teach children to value feelings and individuality rather than trying to fit everyone into the same educational mold. No wonder adults in this society value conformity rather than individuality and freedom!

Ecology

Let's set aside the corporate myth that global warming is not happening and see if we can reverse the effects before it's too late. Let's grow food that is healthy for us – not food that maximizes profit for the rich with fertilizers that poison our soil and our water, and eat holes in our guts. We need to outlaw GMO foods and insist that all food in this country is organically grown

We need to protect our water resources, and provide safe water for everyone. Our prisons need to provide a better method of purifying their water that will not be toxic to the prisoners. Peroxide injector systems are economical and kill toxins without killing the people ingesting the water.

Bankruptcy:

We as a nation are bankrupt financially because we are bankrupt morally. We need to create principles that will give us direction and make our laws consistent with those principles. Our government's job would be to act in accordance with the goals we as a people create.

Every American should be entitled to a job. In fact, we should add the right to paid employment to the Bill of Rights. Our mental health is contingent upon feeling purposeful, and work gives us a sense of purpose. When people feel a sense of purpose, they do not look to escape via drugs or alcohol. Crime rates will go down as people feel more in control of their lives. We can recreate a manufacturing economy in this country and stop importing everything we use. Dependency creates feelings of hopelessness. Self-sufficiency creates optimism.

We spend more than half our national budget on defense and war-related expenses. Let's stop our meddling in other countries' business. Our foreign policy has been directed too long by private interests. We have enough problems here. It's time we spend that money on bettering our country. Let's start a civilian job corps and build a democracy.

Profit-Sharing:

Persons owning businesses should be sharing profits with their employees. They didn't make those profits alone and those who helped should be rewarded for their efforts. In companies with over ten employees, the owner's salary should not exceed ten times that of the lowest paid employee and their profit beyond the first $250,000 should not exceed 30%. The rest of the profit should be shared with the employees. The profit to the owner beyond the first million should not exceed 10%. This alone could create a new cooperative economy where the wealth is shared. This would create a Fair Economy rather than a Capitalist Economy where the wealth is hoarded by the rich. We could give these corporations some time to transition to this system. They can start sharing 10% more of the profit each year until they are left with their 10 or 30%. Employees would have a vote as to whether to take companies public and share their profits with others. Businesses with less than ten employees should give each employee at least 10% of the profit beyond the first $250,000.

It's very nice that some millionaires/billionaires are leaving their money to charity. However, no one really wants charity.

What we want is the dignity of being able to thrive on our own and the possibility of achieving our own dreams.

Healthcare:

The control that pharmaceutical companies have over our healthcare system limits our health. If we focused on preventive care and allowed alternative medicine to be covered by health care policies, we would save millions. Natural antidepressants, for example, which typically work as well or better than prescription medication and have no negative side effects that are going to cause subsequent health problems, typically cost far less than prescription antidepressants. We could save millions on anti-depressants alone!

Of course, we are grossly overusing antidepressants. In the past people expected a certain amount of sadness in life. Sadness comes and goes with life events. Now doctors are treating even situational depression with antidepressants. If left alone, the sadness usually goes away on its own. Therapy can help speed that up.

More and more chronic illnesses are being linked to a lack of good bacteria in the gut caused by the overuse of antibiotics, other medications, parasites, and pollutants. Alternative healthcare can treat illnesses naturally, avoiding damaging chemical medications, and restoring gut health.

There are already alternative cures for many serious diseases, but large portions of the population have been brain-washed by doctors who have said for years that supplements just produce "expensive pee." People should be able to choose whether they want to be treated by a traditional doctor, acupuncturist, or a naturopath, and alternative therapies such as Frequency Specific Microcurrent Therapy, Prolozone Therapy, and other cutting edge treatments should be covered by all insurance policies. If "We the People" (rather than pharmaceutical companies) were in control of health policy, we could make this happen.

We need universal healthcare. Many people are kept out of the workforce by lack of healthcare, when their problems could be cured by either alternative or conventional western medicine. With healthcare, they could return to become productive members of society rather than a drain on society. We should get rid of Workmen's Comp insurance that often delays to the point that people end up with permanent damage.

Of course, the easiest and most logical solution to the healthcare problem would be to extend Medicare to everyone. Just about everything else overburdens the middle class. We need to quit trying to protect the wealthy and take care of the rest of the people of this country.

Social Services Programs:

If we make it our goal to provide the opportunity for every individual to work and contribute to society, then the reform of social services programs are needed as well. If we give everyone the right to work, many people currently on welfare would be happy to work, and we would minimize the number of people we have to support. Some of these people, however, are low functioning intellectually and would need a sheltered workshop situation in order to thrive.

Again, no social service agency should be able to discriminate based on religious beliefs. Counselors working in drug treatment programs and religious programs should not be exempt from the licensing required by other counselors. Parallel is not equal; all people deserve treatment by qualified professionals.

There should be provisions for short-term government disability immediately after a serious disabling accident or illness. People should not have to lose their homes, cars, and dignity before being approved for social security disability. A doctor's note should suffice for short-term disability.

Children are not wage earners and should not be entitled to disability payments. They are already provided with special education programs as well as speech therapy, and sometimes occupational and physical therapy at their schools, and should be granted health insurance as well if the parents are unable to afford insurance on their own. Children with disabilities should be supported by their parents as are all other children. A child's education should not be sacrificed by unscrupulous parents who would handicap their own children for a check. Children should not be trained in not having to earn their income.

People only get satisfaction from earning their way in the world. People who win the lotto typically blow it all within a year or so because they get no sense of achievement from the money or what it buys. When I see these young people who have collected disability as a child at the age of eighteen, they have the expectation that the government should continue to support them as adults, even if their disability was a minor learning problem or attention deficit. Why are we depriving people of the sense of accomplishment achieved by being self-sufficient?

While SSI for children is a well-intentioned program, it's somewhat like taking statin drugs to lower cholesterol. There are just too many unforeseen side effects that outweigh the benefits. It's not that we shouldn't be taking care of children with disabilities. It's just that the delivery system of benefits for children should not be cash. Unfortunately, this is necessary to protect children from parents who would neglect their medical needs or medicate them unnecessarily with psychiatric medications to get the extra income. Any help given to children should be in the form of services. Of course, if the parents were paid a fair wage that they could live on, they might be less prone to sacrifice their children.

Taxes:

Our taxes should be incremental, but fair. The first $250,000 everyone earns should be taxed at no more than 10%. Taxes on income above $250,000 should increase in increments of 5% for each $250,000 up to 25%. So if you made $750,000, you would pay 10% taxes on the first $250,000, 15% on the second $250,000, and 20% on the third $250.000. No one should have to give more than 25% of their earning to the government – even corporations.

I don't believe large corporations need a tax break more than the rest of us do. There's no proof that the tax breaks encourage corporations to hire more people. As others have pointed out, there is evidence that it encourages larger bonuses to the big wigs and expensive group vacations in the guise of staff development/teambuilding retreats.

While small businesses should be a path out of poverty regardless of a person's education level, high taxes on those small businesses make it difficult to survive, serving to protect large businesses from competition. Thus, covert businesses like drug sales and prostitution flourish as the easier path to success. If anyone should get a tax break, it should be people building small businesses, who will create more jobs as they expand. While I pay 30% in taxes and FICA, about 30% of my income also goes to expenses, leaving me with a fraction of what I actually earn as a small business person. How much does Exxon pay in taxes? Isn't it 0%?

Inheritance taxes should allow a generous tax-free five million dollars to each heir. Anything left after that would revert to the government as a tax. This would, in effect, provide an end to an aristocracy which believes it is superior and entitled to special treatment by the fact of being born into wealth, and which enjoys undue influence on our government policies. Of course, we'd have to set a limit on how many heirs a person could have or they could all arrange to leave money to each other's children.

House taxes should be a one-time tax just like everything else we buy. We can either pay that tax at the time of purchase or spread it over the length of the mortgage. When we're done paying for the house, we should be done paying the taxes on the house. The property is then ours and no one can take it from us. Then we will not be left struggling to pay never-ending taxes when we retire.

Interest rates:

Currently, people with the least money are charged the highest interest rates, keeping the poor where they're at. While there have been some regulations put in effect recently to control when banks and credit cards can raise our interest rates, there still seems to be no limit on how high those rates can go. There should be a limit on the interest that can be charged! The banks should not need to charge us more than five percent above the interest rate they pay us on our savings accounts. That should be ample to support a bank. Mortgage companies and credit cards should not need more than five percent either. Even though we have bailed out these large banks, they still do not want to pay us any interest on our savings. I think they'd start paying us some interest if they could only charge us 5% more than they pay us.

Social Security Retirement:

I believe in social security. People with limited funds will not typically voluntarily put those funds in a retirement plan. People with limited funds will not leave those funds in the retirement plan if they lose their jobs, get injured, or even have a good idea for investing that money. The government has been doing to us what we might do ourselves if given a chance – take that money out of there before we retire. And they don't give it back to us!

Our social security accounts should be like individual retirement accounts. The only person who should be able to take out that money is the person who put the money in there – or the heirs if they die before it's gone. And we should be able to decide at what age we want to retire based on the money we were able to put in, the interest we've earned, and the income that would give us. We could contribute more than we are required if we are able and our employers could also contribute into our accounts. Separate employee retirement accounts would not be needed, protecting us from losing that retirement if our employer has a mishap.

Supplemental income or SSI should be provided to those who have not been able to save enough money in their social security accounts to retire. While people have been talking for some time about having a $15 an hour minimum wage, we need to also recognize that the elderly also need a minimum wage of that same $30,000/year.

Currently, people who work all their lives and retire on social security alone struggle to survive right along with those people who have never worked or worked minimally. With their SSI checks, low-income housing, and food stamps, persons who have never worked or who have worked minimally end up making as much as the retired workers do with their Social Security payments. Those of us who have worked all of our lives and paid enormous amounts into Social Security are now being told we have to wait longer to retire, and are made to feel we are a drain on society that the younger generation has to support. They should not have to support us! We paid in a lot of money! Invested anywhere else, we could have millions to retire on.

Those of us who have spent our lives paying into social security should be paid back the funds the government took out for other purposes. The government owes us with interest and we should not have to spend our final days in poverty. If we cut back the war spending, we would have ample funds for everything else. There needs to be a paper trail for the bottomless pit of Department of Defense spending. We can no longer tolerate that our money is being spent secretly in ways no one has to account for while we struggle to survive.

Unemployment:

Rather than paying government-funded unemployment, we can have work programs for everyone who cannot find their own jobs. People who can't find jobs on their own would be able to join a work co-op, a civilian job corps. All of these work programs would have the goal of becoming self-supporting; profits would be shared among the workers.

Professional Licensing

Currently, professionals are licensed by the state in which they work, and moving to another state is akin to moving to a foreign country. Each state has its own requirements for teachers, mental health professionals, and lawyers. Moving to another state may mean taking additional courses and certainly another state exam. Whose needs are being served by controlling professionals in this way? If we're going to restrict people's freedom in this country, we need to have a good reason to do so. We are one country and should have licensing which extends to all fifty states. This way, professionals could easily move to areas of greater need.

Foreign Policy:

We need to create a Peace Department and give the world the message that peace is our goal. We need to help make the United Nations rather than the United States the major arbiter in foreign disputes and the major peacekeeper militarily. This way we can help make the world as a whole a democracy and put a check on the corporate interests that currently direct our foreign policy. In doing so, we'll gain the respect of the rest of the world.

Becoming Agents of Change

I have presented my own ideas of what I believe can enable our country to grow into true greatness. It is my hope that everyone who reads this book will submit their ideas to their representatives and demand change. Together we can build a stronger, more caring and just society.

The best way to find yourself is to lose yourself in the services of others.

Mahatma Ghandi

Love is the only force capable of transforming an enemy into a friend.

Rev. Martin Luther King, Jr.

Addendum

This addendum provides an explanation of the state of moral deviation which characterizes a rigid, fundamentalist perspective. This review of literature may not be of interest to all readers. However, I have not come to the conclusions I have arrived at on my own, and would like to give credit to those who helped me.

Moral certainty is always a sign of cultural inferiority. The more uncivilized the man, the surer he is that he knows precisely what is right and what is wrong. All human progress, even in morals, has been the work of men who have doubted the current moral values, not of men who have whooped them up and tried to enforce them. The truly civilized man is always skeptical and tolerant, in this field as in all others. His culture is based on "I am not too sure."

H.L. Mencken

Moral Development

From Dualistic Exclusivity to Relativistic Inclusion

To understand the shortcomings of fundamentalist morality, we need to look at the process of moral development. A number of researchers have over the years attempted to map the development of cognition and a somewhat parallel development of morality throughout the life span.

Piaget documented cognitive development from concrete thinking to a capability for abstract thinking. Young children think in concrete terms, and with maturation may develop the ability to comprehend abstractions. Some of us develop this capacity far better than others. Most adults I have interviewed over the years for social security evaluations are still very concrete in their thinking. When I ask them to interpret the saying, "People in glass houses should not throw stones," they reply, "They'll break their house." When extremely concrete people are asked, "What brought you in today?" they respond, "my car" or "the city bus."

The process of identity formation involves the creation of a cognitive map or network of presuppositions, premises and expectations that make up the way we perceive the world. This mental map is composed of schemata which organize our past experiences and serve to reduce the complexity of the undifferentiated mass of incoming information.

Cognitive structures form as dichotomous polar opposites which tend to be simplistically categorized as good or bad. According to Kelly, as we grow cognitively, our cognitive structure becomes more differentiated, resulting in a continuum between polarities rather than discrete categories, moving from a dichotomous style to a more relativistic style.

One of the tasks of adolescence contributing to identity formation is the achievement of the coordination of multiple perspectives. This empowers young adults to think about possibilities rather than simply the reality of the here and now – to think abstractly. Good decision-making requires this ability to conceive of alternative possibilities.

Several other factors have been identified in distinguishing between cognitive styles. Studies of authoritarianism by Adorno et al. looked at the openness or closedness of a person's belief system. The authoritarian personality is rigid, conforming, intolerant of ambiguity, and authority-dependent. Authoritarianism is characterized by a rejection of opposing beliefs, a tendency to see things in black and white, and a relatively low degree of interconnectedness among belief systems.

Rotter examined cognitive style in terms of internal and external locus of control. Individuals with an internal locus of control perceive what happens in their lives to be the result of their own behavior and those with external locus of control attribute events to luck, chance, fate, or other people. Thus, those with external locus of control do not recognize their power to affect their own lives.

Vannoy identified three broad classes of information processing that reflect cognitive simplicity: a tendency to focus on very few stimulus dimensions in decision-making while excluding others, a tendency to make gross black and white distinctions between positions on any one stimulus dimension, and a tendency to value a highly ordered existence while viewing ambiguity as a threat.

Wilkinson and Schwartz found cognitive styles of dualism and relativism to be related to authoritarianism and locus of control. Persons with a dichotomous cognitive style tend to be authoritarian and attribute the rewards in their lives to factors external to themselves. Persons with a relativistic cognitive style on the other hand, have open rather than authoritarian belief systems and tend to attribute the rewards in their lives to their own actions.

In a study of Harvard men, Perry noted a progression from an initial dichotomous position characterized by polarities of right/wrong and good/bad to one of greater relativism in which it is understood that truth is relative, and the meaning of an event depends on the context in which it occurs.

According to Perry, dualists tend to believe that knowledge is either good or bad, true or false. They believe that correct answers exist for problems and look to authorities to provide the answers to these problems. Relativists view knowledge on a continuum;

knowledge is neither right nor wrong, but is evaluated according to such factors as context, consistency, and logical relations.

Perry noticed major developmental shifts from *dualism* to *multiplicity* to *relativism* in male Harvard students. Development begins from an initial position that Perry calls basic duality, in which the individual views the world in polarities of right/wrong, and good/bad. There is one right way to do things. All knowledge is known by authorities who are depended on to teach right from wrong. As the student comes to understand that authorities may not have the right answers, the student enters a position of multiplicity. From the position of multiplicity, there is no longer one truth, but an infinite number of possible truths. While the student recognizes multiple points of view, there is still a search for the right answer. When a position of full relativism is attained, the individual comes to the understanding that truth is relative, and that the meaning of an event depends on the context in which the event occurs and on the framework that is used to understand that event. Perry's final stage is one of commitment in the face of relativism.

In Perry's scheme there is a clear sequential and hierarchical ordering of positions. Perry's sample was a relatively homogenous group and this linear sequence of development stood out clearly when the context in which development occurred was held constant. The educational process at Harvard appears to promote relativistic thought. Most people attending Harvard come from advantaged backgrounds with opportunities for growth not available to lower socio-economic groups. The term "development" used by Perry implies value with relativism being at a higher or better level than dualism.

In Belenky's study, where context was allowed to vary, universal developmental sequences were far less obvious. Belenky, Clincy, Goldberger, and Tarule studied the cognitive development of women from a broader range of socio-economic situations and ethnic backgrounds than Perry's Harvard sample. Belenky et. al. described perspectives from which women know and view the world, and left it up to future research to determine whether these perspectives have any stage-like qualities. It became apparent through their research however, that women do shift from one stage to another during the course of their lives, although the precipitants of the shifts and the ages at which they occur varied. They developed five major epistemological categories:

1. Silence: a position in which women experience themselves as mindless and voiceless, and subject to the whims of external authority. Women at this stage are passive, reactive, and dependent, and their thinking tends to be limited to concrete and specific. They see life in terms of polarities, and believe the source of self-knowledge is in others, not in themselves.

2. Received knowledge: a perspective from which women conceive of themselves as capable of receiving, and even reproducing, knowledge from all-knowing external authorities, but do not see themselves as capable of creating knowledge on their own. These women, like those in a position of silence, think in terms that are concrete and dualistic. As in Perry's position of basic dualism, they assume that there is only one right answer to each question; truth is absolute. They have little confidence in their own ability to speak, believing that truth comes from others. They are intolerant of ambiguity, take things literally, and like predictability and clarity. These women collect facts, but do not develop opinions. Facts are seen as truth, while opinions don't count. Women at this stage tend to use the words "should" and "ought." They define themselves in terms of concrete social and occupational roles. Their either/or thinking makes it difficult to express notions of becoming. They tend to equate occupational changes with changes in the self.

3. Subjective knowledge: a perspective from which truth and knowledge are conceived of as personal, private, and subjectively known or intuited. There is still the perception that there are right answers; however, the source of truth has shifted from external to internal. These women are their own authorities; they have discovered that firsthand experience is a valuable source of knowledge. They see themselves as conduits of intuited truth rather than constructors of it, while viewing truth as unique to each individual.

Developmentalists such as Piaget, Erikson, and Kohlberg have noted this shift from external to internal authority as one of the central tasks of adolescents. These women are often characterized by what Erikson termed a negative identity – they define themselves in opposition to others. As in Perry's stage of multiplicity, truth is no longer conceived as absolute and singular, but multiple and infinite.

4. Procedural knowledge: a position in which women are invested in learning and applying objective procedures for obtaining and communicating knowledge. They now use reasoned reflection, acknowledging that intuition may deceive. The inner voice turns critical of their ideas. Knowledge is seen more objectively – as a process. These women tend to be practical, pragmatic problem-solvers.

5. Constructed knowledge: a position in which women view all knowledge as contextual, experience themselves as creators of knowledge, and value both subjective and objective strategies for knowing. There is an integration of thinking and feeling with a high tolerance for internal contradiction and ambiguity. At this stage it is believed that "all knowledge is constructed and the knower is an intimate part of the known." These women are seriously preoccupied with the moral or spiritual aspects of their lives, and strive to translate their moral commitments into action. There is a sense of responsibility to the larger community. They aspire to work that contributes to empowerment and improvement in the quality of life of others.

In the Belenky study, women at low socio-economic levels seemed to fall toward the dichotomous end of the continuum. Variables related to the development of cognitive style included parenting style, life experiences, and formal education. Silent women frequently described their parents as chaotic or unpredictable. All of the women in this group experienced some form of gross neglect and physical and/or sexual abuse by one or more parent. More often than not, at least one parent was alcoholic. Often it was the eventual reaction to sexual abuse which brought the women out of silence.

Parents of received knowers used predominantly one-way conversations; the parents talked and the children listened. Subjective knowers grew up in families that were less advantaged, more permissive, or more chaotic than average. The shift into subjectivism generally seemed more a reaction to a failed male authority rather than the exposure to diversity of opinion that Perry observed as a catalyst to shift out of authority dependent dualism. There was a crisis of trust where women had to rely upon themselves rather than the men in their lives. However, women with socioeconomic backgrounds similar to the men in Perry's study, tended to follow the same path as the men, growing into subjectivism through education.

The descriptions of chaotic activity, alcoholism, violence, and abandonment were sharply diminished in stories told by procedural and constructivist knowers. While 75% of silent and received knowers depicted one or both of their parents as alcoholic, only 6% of the procedural and constructivist knowers combined gave a parent this label. While a few of these women had parents who were separated or divorced, none of the fathers abandoned the father-daughter relationship – an event that occurred frequently among the first three categories. There was a tendency on the part of women in the early categories to allocate intellectual capacities to fathers and emotional ones to mothers. Only the constructivists were likely to see mothers and fathers as possessing both intellectual and emotional capacities.

So both Perry in his studies of male students and Belenky et al. in a study of women found a range of cognitive styles from dichotomous thinking characterized as a concrete stage with little tolerance for ambiguity, rigid beliefs, and an external source of knowledge and authority to more relativistic thinking in which we trust our internal feelings, have a tolerance for ambiguity, a flexible belief system, and an awareness of process.

Cognitive style has implications for style of moral reasoning as well. Kohlberg, in his study of boys and men, developed a theory of moral development which reflects a dichotomous cognitive style where an absolute right or wrong is recognized. Kohlberg found that moral development evolved from following the dictates of an external authority to a position where one's own internal authority is followed. The capacity for moral reasoning also follows the development of cognition from concrete to abstract thinking. At the initial level that Kohlberg labels "pre-conventional," rules are complied with to avoid punishment and to serve one's own interests. At the next level, the "conventional level," people follow rules in conformity with stereotypical images of good behavior; there is an orientation to doing one's duty and maintaining the social order for its own sake. At the highest or "post-conventional" level, abstract laws and universal principles are relied upon to adjudicate disputes and conflicts between conflicting claims impersonally and fairly. The emphasis is upon justice with capacity for justice being dependent upon one's level of cognitive development. While this higher level of development represents a move from the concrete to the ability to apply abstract principles, it still implies an inner sense of absolute right and wrong, characteristic of a dichotomous rather than a relativistic cognitive style.

Gilligan, from her study of women, takes her theory of moral development a step further. She believes that due to their different socialization, women develop another approach to morality.

Women's conceptions of self are rooted in a sense of connection and relatedness to others. Moral development for women is organized around notions of responsibility and care. This contrasts with the development of men, who tend to define themselves in terms of separation and autonomy, and develop more of a rights orientation.

For Gilligan, moral development begins from a point of acting out of self-interest, moves to a point of self-sacrifice, putting other's needs before one's own, and finally, to balancing one's own needs with those of others. The context of moral choice is important; the needs of individuals cannot always be deduced from general rules and principals. Because the emphasis is on context rather than absolute notions of right and wrong, this moral style reflects a relativistic cognitive style.

Carl Jung's theory of personality types also offers an explanation of differences in cognitive and moral styles – specifically in the way people perceive the world and the way they make judgments or come to conclusions. A personality test reflecting Jung's theory was created by Isabel Briggs Myers. In this test, the concrete/abstract and dichotomous/relativistic factors are separated into two continua. The *Sensing-Intuition* scale of the Myers-Briggs Type Indicator (MBTI) represents a continuum between concrete and abstract thought. The *Judging-Perceiving* scale of the MBTI represents a continuum between dichotomous and relativistic thinking. A positive correlation exists between scores on the *Sensing-Intuition* and *Judging-Perceiving* scales. Briggs Myers did not posit a directionality of development in type other than to say that in later life we tend to develop our weaker functions.

According to Jung, there are two distinct ways of perceiving. One is the process of *Sensing* through which the individual becomes aware of things directly through the five senses. The other is the process of *Intuition*, an indirect perception by way of the unconscious. The frequency of *intuitive* types in the general population is considerably less than the incidence of *sensing* types. According for the Center for the Application of Psychological Type, *Intuitives* are roughly estimated as *26-34%* of the population. *Sensing* types eclipse the *Intuitives* with *66-74%* of the population.

Most *sensing* types rely on experience rather than theory, and trust the conventional and customary way of doing things. They like doing what is familiar to them rather than learning new things. Most *intuitive* types rely on inspiration rather than past experience and are interested in the new and untried. They sometimes find complex ideas coming to them as a complete whole, unable to explain how they knew.

There are also two attitudes towards judging or coming to conclusions. *Perceiving* includes the processes of becoming aware of things, people, occurrences, and ideas. *Judging* includes the processes of coming to conclusions about what has been perceived. Together perception and judgment govern much of outer behavior because perception determines what people see in a situation and their judgment determines what they decide to do about it. These attitudes are mutually exclusive and cannot be used at the same time. In order to come to a conclusion, people have to use the *Judging* attitude and have to shut off perception for the time being. When using the *Perceptive* attitude, people have to shut off judgment and remain open to the possibilities that exist.

People with a *Judging* preference are apt to feel a sense of urgency until a decision has been made. People with a *Perceiving* preference tend to be resistant to making a decision, feeling there's never enough data to make a decision. *Judging* types are organized and systematic; they live in a planned, orderly way, aiming to regulate life and control it. *Perceptive* types are more curious and open-minded; they go through life in a flexible, spontaneous way, aiming to understand life and adapt to it. While

Judging types spend a great deal of time organizing their lives and the world they live in, *Perceiving* types just live their lives. *Judgers* plan their work and work their plan while *Perceivers* go with the flow.

The *Judging-Perceiving* preference reflects the continuum between dualistic and relativistic thought processes. *Judgers* tend to think dichotomously and are uncomfortable with ambiguity. For *Judgers*, there's a right way and a wrong way to do anything. They have a tendency to make judgments or decisions on limited information and stick with that decision rather than responding to new information which might change their decision. *Perceivers*, on the other hand, have a tendency to keep collecting new information rather than drawing conclusions or judgments (making decisions) on any subject. *Perceivers* see many shades of grey rather than black and white dichotomies. An estimated 55-60% of the general population in the United States is Judging and 40-45% are Perceiving.

It is difficult to distinguish between some characteristics of the Sensing-Intuition scale and the Judging-Perceiving scale, which together reflect a continuum between concrete/dichotomous and abstract/relativistic thinking.

Research on the Sensing-Intuition scale has shown:

1. *Intuitive* persons are more likely to be at a higher level of conceptual development.

2. There is a positive relationship between academic comfort and *Intuition* as well as a relationship between low academic comfort and *Sensing* preference.

3. *Sensors* tend to be attracted to practical vocations. They place a high value on authority and work. *Sensors* like to proceed orderly toward well-defined goals.

4. *Intuitives* like to use their minds and have a considerable tolerance for complexity. They generally express a strong need for autonomy and have a positive attitude toward change.

5. Myers found 79% of male gifted students and 88% of female gifted students to be *Intuitive* types.

6. *Sensing* types fall near or below the mean in IQ for their classes, and the Intuitive types fall near or above the mean.

7. *Sensors* are more frequently found in special education classes.

8. Studies of creative people found creativity to be associated primarily with *intuition* and secondarily with *perception*.

Little was found on research on the Judging-Perceiving scale that was not also true of the Sensing-Intuition scale.

1. *Perceptive types* express a strong need for autonomy

2. *Perceptive* types enjoy change and have a high tolerance for complexity.

3. For women, academic comfort was found to be related to a *perceiving* attitude.

Myers and Myers hypothesized that the correlations between the *Sensing-Intuition* and the *Judging-Perceiving* scales reflect real world relationships. *Sensing* types who rely on past experience are more likely to prefer order and predictability while *intuitive* types who are attuned to new possibilities are more likely to seek openness to change. Part of the process of making good decisions involves generating alternative courses of action and evaluating these. Coming up with new ideas involves creativity. In order to access creative intuition, one must be able to suspend judgment (the categorization of information into good/bad dichotomies), and use passive volition, letting go and allowing the desired phenomena to happen. Research shows the following:

1. *Sensing* and *Judgment* have been related to left brain dominance while *Intuition* and *Perception* are most prevalent with right brain dominance.

2. High aptitude is correlated with *Intuition* and *Perception* while high achievement is correlated with *Intuition* and *Judging*. *Judgers* tend to be overachievers and may get higher grades than *Perceptive* types in spite of lower aptitude.

3. *Judging* and *Sensing* preferences have been found to be associated with obsessive personality traits.

4. *Intuitives* and *Perceivers* have been found to favor nontraditional, personally articulated ethical preferences that are case-specific and based on abstract criteria. *Sensors* and *Judgers* prefer traditional, rule-guided principals derived from unambiguous axioms that apply in the same way to everyone.

From this it can be seen that people who are *Sensing* and *Judging* would be more apt to be comfortable in fundamentalist churches, where there is a clear dictate of what is right and wrong, and a clear and easy path to heaven (join the club and comply with what church authorities tell you to do). *Sensing/Judgers* believe in "one right way," while *Intuitive/Perceivers*, who can tolerate ambiguity, can conceive of many paths which might be equally good. The idea that there could only be one right way seems nonsensical to them. There are shades of grey everywhere.

According to the website for the Center for the Application of Type, 66-74% of the US population is *Sensing* and 54-60% are *Judging*. Persons with the *Sensing-Judging* combination are naturally conservative by nature and crave stability. Oswald and Kroeger found that persons with combined *Sensing* and *Judging* personality traits made up 40% of the US population. It has been estimated that 75% of persons attending "traditional" churches have *Sensing-Judging* traits.

I believe everyone starts out with an *Intuitive* and *Perceiving* nature. *Sensing* and *Judging* are distortions of our natural state. Children are by nature curious and creative, but authoritarian parenting, chaotic lifestyles, cultish religions, and a school system based on memorizing rather than thinking and creating distort many into extreme *Sensing* and *Judging* perspectives. Perhaps as Kolberg found, a proper liberal arts education can correct this to some extent. *This may be our only hope.*

Carl Jung identified two kinds of conscience:

1. Moral conscious involves an instinctive desire to conform with the norms and expectations of society with an aversion to anything new. This is problematic since external moral laws generally represent repressive social forces engineered by the powerful to preserve their privilege. They serve the needs of those who create them. Yet we internalize these mores of our society in the form of the moral consciousness.

2. Ethical conscience arises when there is a consciousness of a choice between two ways of acting or deciding. Jung suggests that if the conflict is held in consciousness, the creation of a third standpoint may emerge representing a creative solution to the conflict of duties. However, one would need to have some tolerance of ambiguity to be able to do this.

When we fail to conform to society's norms, we not only experience disharmony with society at large, but with our conscience within. Conscience is a dialectical process between consciousness and the unconscious. It is the means by which we make moral evaluations.

Jung posited that our decision-making ranges across a continuum from *Thinking* to *Feeling,* a third factor in the Myers-Briggs Type Indicator. *Thinkers* approach decision-making in a rational, logical manner, while the *Feeler's* decision-making is more value-centered. *Thinkers* tend to focus on differences between people while *Feelers* tend to look for commonalities between people. *Thinkers* focus on obtaining their own goals while *Feelers* are more interested in keeping the peace and making others happy.

The driving force behind the conscious is our feelings. Jung believed we need to use both feeling and thinking functions to make good decisions. To Jung, intellectualism (the exclusion of feeling) is antithetical to a moral attitude. Feeling is the means by which we relate to and grasp the moral significance of an event. Nonconscious experiences, including feelings and intuitions, yield ethical knowledge. We can verify these hunches experientially, giving us some sort of knowledge of what is moral. Studies have suggested that individuals with strong *Intuitive* and *Feeling* functions may be likely to reach a higher level of moral development. Women tend to score higher on both *Intuition* and *Feeling* on the MBTI. Thus, we need more women making decisions in this country.

Jung posits that codified norms, laws, and customs are *immoral* if held to be *literal*. This statement clearly suggests that concrete, dichotomous thinking is morally inferior to abstract, relativistic thinking. The directionality of development may be unclear and growth may be somewhat of a dialectical process, but the more humane, kind, intelligent stance involves relativistic thinking.

Looking at cognitive styles, fundamentalism is characterized by a simplistic, dichotomous style which makes gross black and white distinctions between positions and views ambiguity as a threat. They have an external locus of control and externalize their battles of conscience, saying it was the devil that made them do evil and God who rewarded them with their many children. They are authoritarian, looking to the church as the source of knowledge of what is moral rather than listening to their own inner voice.

This kind of thinking has resulted in our great passivity and our current out-of-our-control government. We need to start educating parents and revising our school system to encourage the development of a more relativistic, compassionate cognitive and moral style. Peace on our planet depends on it.

Conclusion

When I was supervising interns in a prior life, they always commented on how comfortable I seemed among the insane in locked mental health units. I told them that I knew the only thing that separated me from those psychotic people was my ability to question the thoughts that came into my head. Persons with Schizophrenia do not question the insane voices they hear. They think the voices come from an infallible source, and allow them to rule them.

I think as a whole, the people of this country have been much like the psychotic people in that locked unit. We have blindly followed what our leaders have told us, telling ourselves we are the best country in the world – unquestionably on the "right" side of every battle our leaders want us to fight. We've allowed unjust laws to be passed in the name of justice. We've allowed banks to rob us and pharmaceutical companies to dictate medical practices. For years pharmaceutical companies have been trying to regulate people's right to treat themselves with natural substances and have been very near to taking away that freedom.

We, the working people of this country, have been giving and giving, while neglecting our own needs. We have been so busy working and struggling to survive that we have not stopped to think about our own needs, who we want to be, or where we want to go as a nation. We have allowed ourselves to be ruled by laws that make no sense to anyone but those who profit from them. This country needs to stop, define itself, and collectively decide where we want to go.

Long ago, I put a quote on my office wall. It said, "If you don't know where you're going, you're going to end up somewhere you don't want to be." I think we all recognize that we're at a place we don't want to be at as a nation. We need to create a new mission statement for this country and make all of our policies consistent with that mission rather than having the mish-mash of laws we have now, which only benefit the wealthy. We need to make our prisons and social service programs self-supporting. We need to provide jobs for everyone that can work.

We need to teach our children to think so that they will do better than we have done in monitoring what our government does.

We can create a committee for the rewriting of our government policy and our economic system. This committee should be a multidisciplinary team of experts, who should be open to suggestions from everyone in our nation. The internet provides the opportunity for every citizen to give input into our new mode of government. The committee should review all suggestions and develop proposals for a new system to be voted on by all of us.

We need to approach fundamentalists with compassion. They are in a different kind of prison with bars created by a painful, distorted belief system. We need to help them see the folly of their belief system and raise awareness that they are but pawns of the wealthy who seek to control them through their religion. At the same time, we must not tolerate their deceit and protect ourselves from their attack on our way of life. If we define evil as intentionally trying to harm people, then this movement is definitely evil.

We need to organize ourselves at the grassroots level to maintain our freedom, which is daily being eroded. The Christian Taliban is expanding very quickly. When voting for public officials, we must consider that many of them (especially Tea Party Members) are promoting the Taliban, and know that voting for anyone who wants to suppress women's reproductive rights is not just voting against reproductive rights, but also likely against the existence of many other basic rights, including equal wages, educational and work opportunities, and even the right to vote. We must exert pressure on our elected officials to keep any more of these fundamentalists out of the Supreme Court of our land.

While we must have compassion for those deceived by religious lies, we need to recognize that there are no harmless fundamentalists. They do not believe in "live and let live." My punishment has not stopped with leaving my prison job or even finishing the construction of my house. My business was attacked with my hours reduced to bare survival levels at times prior to being forced to retire. My house has been physically attacked, my privacy invaded, my possessions stolen, my dogs killed, and my health repeatedly attacked. I avoid hiring people to help me out whenever possible as invariably they will sabotage what I ask them to do and steal from me. Since Trump and his hate group cronies were elected, the attacks on my health have increased. This is the work of people who call themselves "Christians."

I have been attempting to sell that house I built in Taliban Territory for some time. But I'm now wondering whether there is anywhere in this country that's safe to live if you're on "the list?"

Only those of us who have had our lives torn apart by these crusaders are acutely aware of what these people can do to our society – what they are currently doing largely unnoticed. Be aware that the Taliban repair person might think it his duty to punish a woman for daring to suggest that she knows what might need to be done and for being bold enough to tell a man what he should do.

We need to help these angry young men see that it is not women working and taking their jobs, which has ruined our economy. As long as our economy is distressed and jobs are scarce, young men and women will continue to enter our voluntary armed forces and help out the rich by fighting their oil wars for them. While the wealth of the top few has exploded over the past few decades, the struggle of the average person has increased proportionately. Fundamentalism encourages putting the blame on women for the struggles of men rather than on our wealthy rulers where it justly belongs.

We need to raise awareness of this movement so that they no longer have the power of invisibility. Hollywood could step forward to help in this area. We need children's television shows depicting the lies put forward by this movement so that kids can be on the lookout for their ploys. We also need educational shows for parents to help their children question authority in appropriate ways. We need to distinguish between politeness, which is warranted, and blind obedience, which is not. High school students should receive parenting training so that they learn to use logical consequences to guide their children rather than using the punishment of authoritarianism.

We need to publish lists of companies which have supported fundamentalist agenda so we can show them our disapproval by shopping elsewhere.

We need to demand disclosure by political candidates of their religious beliefs as they affect their goals politically and their ambitions for our country. Political debates in particular should zero in on Christian Taliban agendas. Theocracies are by nature dictatorships, which history shows us were always in the past corrupt and punitive. If this country becomes a theocracy, independent women will be openly persecuted as I have already witnessed in this state. Law enforcement will offer us no protection. This movement is already actively punishing independent, successful women to scare other women into submission. Women will again be the property of their husbands. Daughters may be raped by law enforcement with the approval of the Church, giving new meaning to the term "legitimate rape." Doctors may butcher women as punishment for their "sins."

God has not been my *punisher* as the fundamentalists like to claim. It has been the fundamentalists who believe they have the one and only interpretation of God's word and God's will, and the arrogance not only to judge, but to *punish* people who disagree with them. This country was founded on religious tolerance and we must not allow this movement to enslave us.

We need to recognize a higher spirituality which holds common threads acknowledged by all the great religions of the world. Our common principals are simple: we should treat people with kindness and compassion, and do what we can to help others in the difficult journey we call life. Just follow the golden rule which says, "Do unto others as you would have them do unto you."

This uber-spirituality, which unites rather than separates the religions, asserts that it is our acts – not our beliefs – which determine our path in the afterlife. We need to recognize that there is no way to judge the validity of our beliefs. Beliefs are something we *choose* to believe largely based on our upbringing in a particular church and the culture we live in. Religions suggest you have to take their declared truths "in faith," acknowledging that there is no way of proving the validity of those beliefs. If there is a judgment day, it makes sense that salvation is not based on your thinking or blind obedience to your religious leaders, but rather on your actions. Religions should follow the creed of "Live and Let Live," acknowledging they have no right to impose their beliefs on anyone else and certainly not harm others.

We need to define a religious institution based on whether it encourages following these unifying principles, and take away the tax exemptions and status as a church of those who do not. An individual's contributions to such an organization should not be deductible either as these are essentially political contributions. These extremists should be recognized as what they are: a political movement and not a religion. We need to have religious tolerance, but only up to the point that a religious group's beliefs lead it to intolerance and to actions intended to hurt others.

Even if we split the country and allowed these terrorists to live their lifestyles within those boundaries, we would not be safe because they believe they need to conquer the world and impose their beliefs on the rest of us.

We have reached a critical age for ensuring that our civilization endures. We need to recognize that there is no one right set of beliefs leading to salvation– only kind and compassionate actions.

Can we hope to see the beginning of a new, more honest and humane era now that we have survived the Mayan end of time? Will we leave the fear and darkness of theocracy and choose the path of love and light? Obviously, it's not going to happen on its own. We need to mobilize now to preserve our freedom and intentionally create the society we want to live in.

It is said that when evil is brought into the light, it will lose its power. It is my hope that this book will bring some light to you so that you may be protected from the deceit and unconscionable *punishment* that has pierced my life.

Religion is regarded by the common people as true, by the wise as false, and by the rulers as useful.

Lucius Annaeus Seneca

My religion is very simple. My religion is kindness.

Dalai Lama

All the commandments…are summed up in this single commandment. You must love your neighbor as yourself.

Jesus

Bibliography

Adorno, T.W., Frandel-Brunswik, E., Levenson, D.J., & Sanford, R.N. (1950). *The Authoritarian Personality*. New York: Harper.

Amen, Daniel G. (2013). *Unleash the Power of the Female Brain*. New York: Harmony Books.

Belenky, M.F., Clinchy, B.M., Goldberger, N.R., & Tarule, J.M. (1986). *Women's Ways of Knowing*. USA: Basic Books.

Bieri, J. (1966). Cognitive complexity and personality development. In Harvey, O.J. (Ed.), *Experience, Structure, &Adaptability (pp. 13-37)*. New York: Springer Publishing Company.

Boone, J. Allen (1943). *You Are the Adventure*. New York: Prentice-Hall.

Byrne, Rhonda (2006). *The Secret*. NY: Atria Books.

Campbell-McBride, Natasha (2010). *GAPS: Gut and Psychology Syndrome*. Amersham: Halston & Co.

Dyer, Wayne W. (2004). *The Power of Intention: Learning to Co-create Your World Your Way*. Carlsbad, CA: Hay House.

Erickson, E. (1959). Identity and the life cycle. *Psychological Issues, 1*, 1-171.

Erickson, E.H. (1963) *Childhood and Society (2nd ed.)*. New York: Norton.

Erwin, T.D. (1983). The Scale of Intellectual Development: Measuring Perry's scheme. *Journal of College Student Personnel, 24*, 6-12.

Gilligan, C. (1982). *In a Different Voice: Psychological Theory and Women's Development*. Cambridge: Harvard University Press.

Goldberg, Michelle (2007). *Kingdom Coming; The Rise of Christian Nationalism*. New York: W.W. Norton & Company.

Goldstein, K.M., & Blackman, S. (1978). *Cognitive Style: Five Approaches to Theory and Research*. New York: Jossey-Bass.

Guilford, J.P. (1980). Cognitive styles: What are they? *Educational and Psychological Measurement,* 40, 715-735.

Hawkins, David (1995). *Power vs. Force.* Sedona, AZ: Veritas Press.

Hedges, Chris (2006). *American Fascists: The Christian Right and the War on America.* New York: Free Press.

Hogan, R. (1970). A dimension of moral judgment. *Journal of Consulting and Clinical Psychology.* 35, 205-212.

Humphreys, Janet K. (1995). The relationship between cognitive style, ethnicity, and level of educational attainment for women receiving Aid for Dependent Children as compared with employed women. Unpublished dissertation.

Joyce, Kathryn (2009). *Quiverfull: Inside the Christian Patriarchy Movement.* Boston: Beacon Press.

Jung, C.G. (1971). *Psychological Types.* (translated by H.G. Baynes, revised by R.F.C. Hull), (Volume 6). Princeton, NJ: Princeton University Press. (Original work published in 1921).

Keating, D.P. (1980). Thinking processes in adolescence. In J. Adelson (Ed.), *Handbook of Adolescent Psychology* (pp.211246). New York: Wiley.

Keirsey, D. & Bates, M. (1978). *Please Understand Me.* DelMar, CA: Prometheus Nemesis Books.

Kohlberg, L. (1969). Stage and sequence: The cognitive developmental approach to socialization. In D. Goslin (Ed.) *Handbook of Socialization Theory and Research* (pp.347-480). New York: Rand McNally.

Kohlberg, L. (1976). Moral stages and moralization: The cognitive developmental approach. In T. Lickona (Ed.), *Moral Development and Behavior: Theory, Research, and Social Issues* (pp. 31-53). New York: Holt, Rinehart, and Winston.

Kroeger, O, & Thuesen, J.M. (1988). *Type Talk.* New York: Bantam.

Lawrence, G. (1982). *People Types and Tiger Stripes, 2nd ed.* Gainesville, FL: Center for the Application of Psychological Type.

Lipton, Bruce H. (2008). *The Biology of Belief.* Carlsbad, CA: Hay

House.

Loevinger, J. (1976). *Ego Development.* San Francisco: Jossey Bass.

Lynn, Barry W. (Ed), (2012). How Air Force rules bar proselytizing by officer. *Church & State,* October, p. 3.

Lynn, Barry W. (Ed.), (2012). Religious right groups undercut anti-bullying programs in schools. *Church & State,* October, p.16.

McCaulley, M.H. (1981). Jung's theory of psychological types and the Myers-Briggs Type Indicator. San Francisco: Jossey Bass, Inc.

Mencken, H.L. (1956). *Minority Report.* NY: Knopf.

Messick, S. (1984) The nature of cognitive styles: Problems and promise in educational practice. *Educational Psychologist,* 19(2), 59-74.

Moore, Michael (2011). *Here Comes Trouble.* NY: Grand Central Publishing.

Myers, I.B. & Myers, P.B. (1980). *Gifts Differing.* Palo Alto, CA: Consulting Psychologists Press.

Perry, W.G. (1968). *Patterns of development in thought and values of students in a liberal arts college: A validation of a scheme.* Cambridge, MA: Harvard University Press. (ERIC Document Reproduction Service No. ED 024 315).

Perry, W.G. (1970). *Forms of Intellectual and Ethical Development in the College Years.* New York: Holt, Rinehart, & Winston.

Perry, W.G. (1981). Cognitive and ethical growth: The making of meaning. In A. Chickering (Ed.), *The Modern American College* (pp. 76-116). San Francisco: Jossey- Bass.

Piaget, J. (1952). *The Origins of Intelligence in Children.* New York: International Universities Press.

Robinson, David W. (2005). *Conscience and Jung's Moral Vision: From Id to Thou.* NY: Paulist Press.

Rokeach, M. (1960). *The Open and Closed Mind.* New York: Basic Books.

Rotter, J.B. (1966). Generalized expectancies for internal vs. external control of reinforcement. *Psychology Monographs,* 80(1),1-28.

Rowen, Robert (2013). New study shows just how dangerous GMO corn is to your body. *Second Opinion,* 23(10), 5-6.

Scherer, Michael and Dias, Elizabeth (2013). After Trayvon. *Time.* July 29, 28-35.

Sharlet, Jeff (2008). *The Family: The Secret Fundamentalism at the Heart of American Power.* New York: HarperCollins Publishing.

Stewart, Katherine (2012). *The Good News Club: The Christian Right's Stealth Assault on America's Children.* NY: Public Affairs.

Tolle, Eckhart (1999). *The Power of Now.* Novato, CA: New World Library.

Van Gelder, H. (1985). *Inner Peace Through the Process of Knowing: Essays in Metapsychology.* NSW, Australia: Robert Martin Outsound Publishing.

Vannoy, J.S. (1965). Generality of cognitive complexity-simplicity as a personality construct. *Journal of Personality and Social Psychology,* 2, 385-396.

Witkin, H.A. & Goodenough, D.R. (1981). *Cognitive Styles: Essence and Origins – Field Dependence and Field Independence.* New York: International Universities Press.

Postscript

The Klan Connection

It was not until after this book was written that I became aware that the people who harassed me while I was working as a prison psychologist, and who have continued my persecution since, are members of the Ku Klux Klan. Having long held the belief that people of color were the primary targets of the KKK, the realization that the KKK also targeted WASP women like myself came as a huge surprise. It was only after the FBI caught three corrections officers plotting to kill someone at one of the prisons where I worked that I began to suspect that the KKK may have also been involved in my harassment. Subsequent research on the internet yielded a Klan greeting that I had once heard my neighbor use while speaking with one of my relatives. My neighbor said, "AYAK," which means "Are You A Klansman?" My relative responded, "AKIA," which means "A Klansman I Am." At the time I heard this exchange, I asked them what those terms meant and was informed that they were a greeting. Still curious, I asked what language it was, at which they burst into laughter and remained elusive.

The Klan connection was further clarified when a former inmate, who had been in confinement at one of the prisons where I had worked, subsequently told me that many of the guards had little nooses hanging from their key chains. What I had long ago sensed was now confirmed – that the power of at least some of the prison employees came not from their prison position, but from their position in some other organization. And with this came the devastating realization that the Ku Klux Klan is that organization. Shocking as this was, given the disproportionate numbers of African-American inmates who have been beaten, tortured, and killed in prison, it made perfect sense.

But the influence of the Klan is by no means limited to our prisons. The Ku Klux Klan, which has in the past been characterized by cross burning and white robes, now appears on the scene as the self-appointed enforcer of the fundamentalist Christian movement. However, its members have dropped the white robes and cross burning for the most part and now seem to prefer working in a stealth manner, harassing those who question their narrow, literal interpretation of the Bible and conservative political beliefs without crediting the Klan for their actions. This persecution now seems to frequently focus on women who may violate their rigid religious laws in any number of ways: getting divorced, having children out of wedlock, getting a "man's" education, taking a good paying "man's" job, having a different sexual orientation, failing to maintain subservience to men, or just having opposing political views.

The overlapping of the KKK and law enforcement in Florida is nothing new. I worked as a social worker in Lake County in the early 70's – shortly after the infamous Sheriff McCall's reign. He was known for telling arrestees with darker skin that they were free to go and then shooting them in the back, saying they were trying to escape. Because of their frequent enmeshment with the KKK, especially in the South, it is imperative that local Sheriff's offices be monitored by the federal government so that people of differing beliefs and skin tones are not denied services or harassed without recourse.

While I had thought that this type of Klan activity had fizzled out for the most part, the "Christian Taliban" and the KKK have been quietly and systematically infiltrating our government agencies, universities, liberal churches and other groups. In the past few years, I have encountered churches which claimed to be liberal, yet told me I was not welcome to attend church or speak there. I attended a women's group which claimed to be about "liberating women," but I was not given the time promised to speak at their meeting, and was told by one of the leaders that I was mistaken – fundamentalist Christianity seeks to *liberate* women.

These hate groups are infiltrating our government with the intent of making this a corrupt "Christian Nation" and punishing anyone who deviates from their narrowly defined religion. There are bills proposed in several states which would give fundamentalists the right to discriminate not just against LGBT

Americans, but unmarried couples, divorced persons, single mothers, and anyone who has had sex outside of marriage. This pretty much gives these radicals the right to discriminate against just about everyone. The children of these "sinners" would also lose their "non-discrimination protections." In Florida the Christian terrorists have long been discriminating against these groups without regard for the law.

Since this book was first published, the chaos in my life has accelerated. I've had more dogs poisoned and my income slashed with eventual forced retirement. The KKK's attempts at intimidation have led me to abandon the SIP home I built in the country. The workers I've hired to do some work on the house so I can sell it have repeatedly sabotaged the job so I have now hired the fifth workers to work on the same thing. Unfortunately, I was met in my new community with yet more terrorist neighbors to continue my harassment.

My unusually bad luck with service people also seems to have followed me to my new home. The electrician I hired to install my surround-sound following my move took the card out of my DVR, told me how wonderful it was, and then announced that "Oops, the DVR won't work anymore since I took out the card." He then proceeded to wire the system backwards with the bass wires going to the front. He insisted on turning the television around to see the back (even though I had cut a large hole in the back of the entertainment center so he could access it from the back) and in doing so, scraped my newly painted entertainment center.

The plumber my neighbor hired to unstop her pipes somehow sent the sewage on to my house. The honest plumber I hired to clean up the mess said it appeared my neighbor's plumber had forwarded the sewage from several houses as much as there was backed up in my cleanout.

I have repeatedly been attacked with high levels of electromagnetic fields (EMF's) since moving to this new house, leaving me with a sensitivity to EMF's. In November 2018, I was forced into retirement by high levels of EMF's at work. Such is the nature of their warfare.

Sadly, this covert war's casualties also include many children. Over the years, I have seen countless children who have been placed in ESE classes because they do not have the glasses they need to read. While some parents may have been willing to sacrifice their children's education for a disability check, I believe the majority of these children with darker skin tones and lighter-skinned children with divorced, unmarried, or LGBT parents are not getting adequate screenings at their schools or are being misinformed about their need for glasses. I've also had parents tell me that their children's pediatricians are denying them referrals to eye doctors in some of these North Florida counties.

I have seen other children whose parents tell me their schools are run by the KKK. Bright children of divorced, never married, or LGBT parents may be made to repeat grades even though they score well above grade level on achievement testing while children who would benefit from special education classes are kept in regular classes, where they repeat grades over and over again.

Other parents have told me of the Salvation Army coming into their disadvantaged neighborhoods and offering free tutoring for their children. This seems like a blessing to parents who cannot afford this luxury, but this blessing does not come without compulsory Bible study. Since the Salvation Army was sued for firing a supervisor who refused to make lists of the gay people in her employ and keep track of which churches her employees attended and how frequently they attended services, it is not unreasonable to assume that the Bible study includes fundamentalist proselytizing that may impact negatively on family relationships.

There is a civil war going on in this country with Christian terrorists conducting a covert attack against citizens who disagree with them. The hidden agenda of many in the Republican Party is to destroy our culture as we know it and establish a totalitarian theocracy, subjugating women to the rule of men and making second class citizens of anyone who will not conform.

We must not let our country be torn apart by lawlessness. This political movement disguised as religion must be stopped from conducting warfare on persons who dare to disagree with them. As has been widely quoted, "The only thing necessary for the triumph of evil is that good people do nothing." So please educate yourselves and those around you as to what's happening in our country so you can be part of a movement to stop it.

About the Author

Dr. Janet Humphreys was born in Akron, Ohio and moved with her family to Argentina at the age of eight. Living just outside the multi-cultural city of Buenos Aires, she was exposed early on to a diversity of political ideas and religious beliefs. An early interest in international relations led her to return to the U.S. and earn an undergraduate major in Political Science at Stetson University. She also pursued studies at the University of Toronto and at York University in Canada, and at the University of New South Wales in Australia.

After working for several years as a social worker and teacher, she continued her studies at Florida State University, and obtained a master's degree in Counseling and Human Systems, and a Ph.D. in Counseling Psychology. She has since worked as a psychologist in the prison system, at mental health centers, and in her own practice, doing disability evaluations for social security.

Her encounters with the Ku Klux Klan and the total lack of protection law enforcement provided led Dr. Humphreys to return to her early political interests and write her story. She recently retired from her psychology practice and hopes to start a center for the study of religious persecution and a refuge for those persecuted by Christian hate groups. She will continue advocating for the reform of the US law enforcement and prison systems, and raise awareness of the dangers posed when religious radicals infiltrate our government, and our separation of church and state is compromised.

God is too big to fit into one religion.

Bumper sticker

I'm for the separation of church and hate.

Bumper sticker

The End